HALFWAY THERE

Lessons at Midlife

ELIZABETH C. HAYNES

This book is a work of nonfiction. Some names and identifying details of people described in this book have been altered to protect their privacy.

ISBN: 978-1-7353023-3-1

Haynes. Elizabeth C.
Halfway There.

Edited by: Amy Ashby

Published by Warren Publishing
Charlotte, NC
www.warrenpublishing.net
Printed in the United States

For Jason, my sunshine.

ACKNOWLEDGMENTS

There are a number of people who helped me on my journey to publishing this book. I ran a crowdfunding campaign through a literary agency to help drum up enough attention to attract a publisher, and none of this would have been possible without the support of my early readers.

Specifically, I would like to thank the following Silver Sponsors: Richard Schaeffer, Judy Parada, Deborah Haynes Brannon, and Dr. Saam Zarrabi of Rodeo Dental & Orthodontics. I would also like to thank the following readers for paying just a little bit extra with their preorder to help me on my way: Sharon Allen, Allan Michael Aquino, Betzi Barden, Amanda Berendsen, India Braddock, Carol Brock, Tamra Bubke, John Burke, Cheryl Charlton, Beth Crosby, Tanvi Dhooria, Sandra Gibbons, Michael and Freda Haynes, Dane Miller, Dr. Cindy Nelson, Brian Price, John Reasner, Rachel Richardson, Patricia Ryan, Becky Schroeder, Robert Sieger, Edyta Skiba, Meghan Stetzik, Michael Taysom, Aishling Tews, Vi Quach-Vu, Audra West and Mick Wist.

VI   ELIZABETH C. HAYNES

Beyond that, I wish to thank the healers in my life. Without their help, I do not believe I would still be here: Dr. Cindy Nelson, Dr. Anne Coleman, Dr. Kenneth Brown, Dr. Richard Herrscher, Cheryl Leo, and Liz Mosesman.

A special note to Dr. Cindy Nelson: You've believed in me, you've helped me, you've encouraged me, you've healed me. I owe you so much gratitude for the impact you've had on my life. You mean more to me than words can express.

A special note to Dr. Anne Coleman: You've never stopped searching for answers. Your brilliance is a force to be reckoned with. What a gift you have! Thank you for all you do for people in this world, and for all you've done for me.

A special note to my husband, Jason: You are the light of my life. You are the best thing that has ever happened to me. I love you, I respect you, I adore you, and I'm blessed by you. I'm grateful for every day we have together. Thank you for supporting me in this journey, and for healing parts of my soul. I'm a lucky girl to have found a true partner in life, and thank you for loving my (our) kitties!

TABLE OF CONTENTS

Moments 1

The Thing about Vacations 7

You're Healthy Until You're Not 14

Life Shows You Your Calling 20

To Wallow Is Human 27

Some People Hate Boundaries 33

Your "Meaningless" Job 38

Finding Confidence When Your Life History Is Contradictive 46

Step Away from the Screen 52

Mornings Are Important 56

Feeling Useful 61

It's Okay to Not Have Kids 66

Finding Meaning in Strange Places 73

Own Your Intro/Extroversion 77

Do Lots of Things 81

Stuff Will Still Bother You 89

There Is Never a Perfect Time 96

Friends Forever? 101

You Don't Have to Do HIIT...108

It's Soulmates (Plural) 114

Not Everyone Grows Up..119

We Have to Transition...124

You Can Read More than One Book..................................129

Boobs Will Sag 137

The Insecure Selfie..142

When Life Doesn't Go as Planned 147

The Lazy River 153

The Morning After...158

Some People Have It Harder than Others..........................162

Jump Off the Bandwagon 167

Cleaning the Bathroom 171

Prejudice Lives Within Us All 176

The Gold Star 185

What Time Is It? 190

I Lost My Hair..194

Peer Pressure...202

Moving On from the Grudge...206

Let's Talk about Bowel Habits 212

Purging Your Attachments 217

The Child Inside...223

Joy Is Attainable 227

Lessons from Lily 233

Home Is … 240

It Takes Courage to Be You...245

AUTHOR'S NOTE

I started writing this book right after I fell off a health cliff, which lasted for more than four years and became one of the darkest periods of my rather traumatic life. I wrote it in spurts, in between varying levels of disability, in an effort to share lessons I thought I might be able to pass on to others. This was my fifth attempt at writing a book in more than a decade, but I knew it was the one I was finally meant to share.

When I was a schoolteacher for a brief period around age thirty, I found my favorite part of the job was relating to my students and sharing in their life struggles. Anything they'd experienced, I'd probably experienced too. And it was in this shared knowing that I felt the most like myself and like I was living an authentic life. I was able to use my hardships and trauma to help others, and I got my first glimpse of meaning for my existence when, previously, there had seemed to be none.

Many of my early writings were emotional vomits penned from a spiral of negativity and pain. This book was created in a different spirit—one of positivity, growth, and understanding. I wasn't able to get there without first getting very sick, and I am grateful for my health challenges (with my hindsight goggles, of course!) because they finally helped me make that shift. I often talk about how we are all on a journey that sometimes doesn't make sense until later, and this book finally gives some meaning to mine.

Thank you for your purchase, and I hope you enjoy my little take on life. These are my most personal stories and I tell them because I think others may see themselves in my experiences and perhaps will feel more empowered to embrace their life as it is—not as it could be, or as it might be. Today is all there is, and there is only one version of us out there. Embrace every day.

MOMENTS

I feel like life is a series of moments, rather than one continuous stream of consciousness that snakes around boulders and over rocks, moving seamlessly down the way. Right now, my moment finds me sitting in the morning light with the sun streaming through my window. It hits the top of my dark wooden desk and reflects brightly toward me in a way that causes me to squint. Everything is quiet except for the occasional singing bird and the low whirr of cars that are speeding down a nearby highway.

I look up from my work to observe an older gentleman walking his dog under the naked winter trees outside my window. Behind me, I listen as my Maine Coon kitty darts around the apartment in his usual post-breakfast mania and my elderly white and orange one settles back down to sleep.

It's just another moment in my life and it will be gone as quickly as it came. I'll get up from my work soon and move on to the next moment in my day, and whether or not this hour of my life registers in my brain for the remainder of my time on earth is hard to say (although documenting it like this sure helps things along in that department). The fact is, we simply can't store all of our moments in easily accessible parts of our brains; this is why we have pictures and journals and people to remind us of what happened and when.

🍃 🍃 🍃

When I was in college, early in the fall semester of my freshman year, I remember lying on my bed alone one afternoon and losing myself in thought and observation as I looked out the open window just above me. The air was still warm from summer, and a faint, humid breeze whispered past my skin. I remember my reclusive roommate was out somewhere doing something or other (probably trying to avoid me) and my suitemates were roaming the campus or in their room studying quietly (I wasn't sure which). But there I was, stretched on top of the covers of my neatly made bed, staring up and out through the old window. It had panes that were crisscrossed by white wooden lines that were also speckled with peeling paint from decades long gone. I looked across the street at the neighboring dorm building, and then I looked upward at the flawlessly blue sky. And I decided to capture that moment in time, consciously, and to hold on to it forever.

I did this by saying to myself, as I surveyed every inch of my dorm room, something like:

Elizabeth, remember this moment. You're young and you're in your first year of college. This moment is here now and pretty soon it won't be. And before you know it, it'll be so far away, you'll wonder what happened to the time. But as you get older, you can always think to yourself, "I remember lying on that bed and capturing that one moment when I was nineteen years old … and holding on to it, always."

It was as if I were imprinting the words onto my soul that were necessary to immortalize that snapshot in time.

The funny thing is, it worked. That was twenty years ago and I still remember it in vivid detail like it was yesterday. I still remember the small room with the white walls and the tiny pedestal sink wedged between a pair of modest armoires and a bathroom door. I still remember the piece of gray carpet we'd picked up as a remnant from a local carpet store, and that we'd carted across town in one hundred-degree temperatures to use as a rug. I still remember my humble desk and chair, where I'd study and write my research papers, and where I'd use my bulky laptop to chat with my friend on this new thing called "America Online" (now known as "AOL"). I also still remember the long, rectangular, black and white TV with the tiny, six-inch screen and the travel handle, which I kept on the edge of the desk to watch at night sometimes, its long antenna reaching halfway to the ceiling and its dials letting me tune in to VHF or UHF.

Mostly, I still remember how it felt to be young and like the world was opening to me in a big horizon, like everything was brand new, like I was finally free, and like I had an entire life stretching beyond that dorm room, that window, that age of nineteen.

I must have been wise beyond my years because I somehow recognized that this moment, like all the others, would soon merge into all the rest. I also understood that I had the power to capture it and hold on to it if I so chose, simply by focusing intently and allowing everything to settle into a permanent place in my mind.

🍂 🍂 🍂

There have been many moments in my life between that one and now. But how many of them do I—or do we, in each of our unique lives—really remember? We always remember the important ones, like the day our cat died or the time we moved into an apartment with our new fiancé. We also remember those that weren't life-changing but were still special in some way, like the time we walked around the neighborhood with our best friend, drinking from a bottle of champagne we'd wrapped in a brown paper bag. But then we remember other seemingly insignificant moments, like the time a cashier at the grocery store was particularly chipper, or the time we were driving down the service road and saw a hawk sitting on the street sign.

I think most of our moments get stuck somewhere inside of us, even though there are millions upon millions of them that we experience in our lifetimes. Because often they can be coaxed out with a photograph, or with a reminder from someone else, or with a journal entry. Or, these days, they're beaten out of us by those "Memories" pop-ups on our social media feeds, which seem so often to be composed of things we'd like to forget.

As I've grown older, every time I've faced a difficult moment—a medical procedure, a job interview, a confrontation with someone I care about—I've tried to remind myself that it's just another moment in my life. "A blip on the radar," as one of my aunts once told me during a particularly difficult time in my life. "It'll come and go just like all the rest."

I sometimes ask myself questions too. Things like: *Have I allowed myself to lose too much energy because of anticipation or regret?* Or, *Have I given more weight to this moment than is appropriate?*

I also sometimes wonder if maybe we should let all of our moments stand as equals, rather than rating them or giving certain ones more weight than others. This doesn't make a lot of sense when we think about joyous moments, because those seem to be automatically elevated in our consciousness. They're part of the good stuff of life. But maybe it does make sense for the moments we perceive more negatively. So maybe it's okay if we don't dwell on what went wrong and instead move toward whatever the next moment may be. And maybe it's okay if we decide to redirect our anxiety about something into a more positive activity we can do to get our minds off things, like taking a walk or baking some bread.

As I move further along in my life, I see that so many moments are lost forever because I didn't record them. And in one sense, this is totally okay and probably the way life was meant to be. But in another, I wish I could remember more of them—if only to validate that I was here at all, because so much of my life is lived inside the walls of my home with only one other human and two cats as a witness.

And yet in a third sense, there are those memories (painful things, life errors, losses, embarrassments) I want to bury and never see again. I try to run away from those moments, but of course they stick the hardest, even though I don't write them down or capture them in a photograph.

Maybe the selective memory is just part of the deal. Part of life. The good with the bad, the strong memories with those that have been forgotten. All of it making up the fabric of time that we experience in blips while we're on this earth to do something more.

THE THING ABOUT
VACATIONS

There's a song by Loverboy that talks about how we all work for the weekend. And isn't that the truth? We spend our lives working and then reward ourselves with tiny bits of quiet: weekends, vacations, sleeping in (on occasion). We'll rest when we're dead … or when we retire, we think. (Although many of us don't have the luxury of that dream anymore.)

I remember very clearly the moment I realized I'd fallen into this expected and pre-scripted rhythm of adulthood. I was at my then mother-in-law's house on a Friday night, already changed out of my work clothes and leaning back in a beat-up chair. I'd just finished my first week at my first full-time corporate job at the tender age of twenty-three. I was paid, although not all that much, to get dressed in a skirt and pantyhose and then be held against my will in a cubicle for eight hours a day as a temp worker. That evening was my first-ever weekend's respite. I sat in that beat-up chair in that beat-up house in quiet observation, listening to the sounds of traffic outside, watching the light in the window turn golden orange, and analyzing my current situation.

I was tired in a way I hadn't experienced before—that was the first thing I noticed. My brother-in-law was playing a video game while my mother-in-law pulled dinner together in the next room—that was the second thing. Everyone seemed rather subdued and weary while all of this was happening—that was the third thing. And the fourth thing I noticed was a sort of collective sigh in the air as all of humanity was transitioning into the weekend, looking forward to the brief bit of time they could control.

This is what people do, I remember thinking to myself rather resolutely. *We work all week long and then we just have the weekends. That's how it's going to be now. I'm doing what everyone else does.*

My feelings about this were mixed at this early time in my life. I felt dismayed by the realization that I was now past the age where I could take a 2:00 p.m. class or sleep in on Fridays, but I was also rather stoic (and a little proud); I had finally joined the ranks of real adulthood after working so hard in college.

⊗ ⊗ ⊗

Now that I'm many more years into my journey, I can say that I've had periods of frustration about being so busy on a day-to-day basis, so strapped for time, so overextended and unable to meet all my obligations or do all my chores—or have any time to myself. This was especially true when I was a mother to a young child and working a full-time office job. I felt so isolated in my struggles because I had nobody to commiserate with, but these days I see how many other people go through these work-life balance difficulties too.

And I ask myself, *how often do we feel this way and actually decide to do something about it? How often do we examine even the smallest ways in which we can take control of our spinning lives?*

I asked myself these questions in my early thirties when I left my corporate job to try to forge my way as an independent. But my new career path opened up a whole other can of worms around financial security, stability, and a different form of exhaustion. So now I'm asking myself those same questions again as I try to merge two worlds—the world where I have a steady job and a steady paycheck, and the world where I really need some flexibility so I can have more time to take care of myself.

I think for some of us, the answer to regaining control is: I'm never going to do anything about my job situation (or, I can't). For others, the answer is: sometimes I try to do something to improve my work-life balance. And still for others, the answer is: I'll do something about it when I have a mental breakdown and finally call in sick, then schedule a vacation. I know it's easy to get pulled back into the machine but I have to wonder, why do we live our lives this way, a solid wall of work with no quiet time in between?

As we all navigate survival in this world, which means having to work one or even two jobs, most of us try desperately to maintain some sort of balance between generating income and living life. One thing I've learned is if you think you can use your weekends as your sole method to recoup, you likely are mistaken.

Many of us pack our weekends so full of activity, they mirror our work weeks and are a poor excuse for a respite. I do think some of us are better at these things than others, though. People who are single and childless (like I was for a long time) are pros at winding down on the weekends because they often are forced to do so. There are no responsibilities pulling at them, nobody else is in the room, nothing is burned into their schedule. Sometimes they fill this time with unhealthy habits such as sleeping too much, consuming excess amounts of wine (guilty), or going out to nightclubs to let their troubles blend away into the smoke (also guilty). But that's a story for another day.

For the most part, I would say single people and those without kids are more likely to do a better job at taking regular "vacations" from the treadmill of life than the rest of us. They have more time to sit quietly with themselves. They also have more time to pursue hobbies that are of interest and that ignite passions within.

But you may be reading this thinking, *I'm single and the last thing I want to be is single. I hate being single. I'm lonely, I'm unfulfilled, I'm isolated.* And I get that. I do. Because I've been there … and it was probably the most depressing time in my life. But if we can get past the feelings of loneliness and transform them into action of some kind—i.e., joining a cooking class or going salsa dancing—then we can find our much-needed vacation moments, even when we feel like the sadness of our lonely lives is constantly draping itself over everything we look at.

🍃 🍃 🍃

As I've gotten older, I've become more in tune with how important it is to take time to get quiet or immerse myself in something I love. I try to make it a regular part of my day, even if it's just during the fifteen minutes I soak in the bath. When humans are going going going, we've got to hit the brakes sometimes and stop for real. And we can't do that just once a year at a fancy tropical resort or by taking a staycation down the street.

All of this is evidenced by how we react when we finally schedule that vacation. Don't we feel awesome? The anticipation, the actual time off, all of it. Once we finally decide to stop thinking about working or obligations or whatever we should be doing instead, we really relax into the positive emotions. The people who never disconnect—even on vacation—have even bigger problems. They don't get to experience the pounding waves inside themselves calming to stillness. Or the dark, tumbling clouds of work and stress and obligations fading away as they reconnect to that part of their personality that appeared more often before they were an adult and had so much weight on their shoulders. Before they no longer had time to imagine and dream and wonder anymore.

The secret is that it doesn't take a vacation to summon those feelings of freedom and happiness. I feel the same way when I spend ten minutes playing with my silly Maine Coon rescue cat, uninterrupted, just focusing on how he leaps through the air after a brown straw mouse. I feel it when I force myself to sit on my meditation cushion in the mornings, after my thoughts finally stop turning over, and I begin coasting in the quiet. It's almost like I'm sitting on a beach.

I also feel it when I watch an old movie on Turner Classic Movies, with Fred Astaire or Bette Davis, or perhaps one of my favorite duos, Myrna Loy and William Powell. It's fun to imagine myself in a different time, far removed from the stressful life I've actually lived (and, admittedly, oftentimes still live). When else? When I read a good book, when I take a walk in nature, or when I spend time with a friend who means a lot to me. I think as human beings, we need as much of this sort of time in our lives as we can shove in. Because the underlying "thing" that is us (our soul, our spirit, whatever) was born in those sorts of moments. Those quiet moments. Those moments of joy.

The nature of our minds is to roll at 100 miles-per-hour all the time. If a quiet moment arises, our minds will find something to fill it with. This is what evolution (media, technology, fast cars, busy cities) is training us to do. So the first step to finding more joy in your life is making sure you schedule down time. Take some time every day to stop, even if it's just for five minutes. Maybe you'll find that those five minutes can turn into ten, which maybe could turn into thirty … on a good day.

The second step is filling those moments with activities that nourish your soul, which may require putting down the smartphone or forcing yourself to sit and look at the trees sway. Really think about what you enjoy, or even what you don't want to do at all during that time (because it stresses you out), and then do (or don't do) that. Try it. You can pick something one day and then try something different the next.

The third step is not losing track of this practice. Because it's easy to get sucked into the swirl when you're stuck in traffic, when you've got to shuffle your kids to the third of five practices, when you've got dinner to make, or when you have a husband to love. Or, conversely, when you feel like you need to wallow in your loneliness, or fill up the quiet in your room (or in your head) with more activity, or swallow some alcohol to numb everything out.

Distractions.

Any spiritual practice requires some form of quiet. Whether it's meditation, prayer, asana, mantras, or listening to a sermon. And this personal time is where we go to reconnect with the meaning of life, isn't it? To find solace, to find a connection, to figure out why we are here at all.

Let's not save our time off just for weekends. Let's not save it just for when we feel like our other obligations will allow us a pass. Let's schedule it in, like lunch. Like coffee. Like that doughnut you love to eat on Friday mornings ... which, to be honest, can be a vacation in and of itself if it means that much to you.

YOU'RE HEALTHY
UNTIL YOU'RE NOT

When we're young (and even sometimes when we're not so young) we think we're invincible. We skip sleep, we work ourselves into exhaustion, we do for our kids until we can't do for ourselves. Sometimes we drown our sorrows in alcohol, or by staying out at clubs until 2:00 a.m., or by running from place to place so that we don't have to sit alone at home with our thoughts.

🍃 🍃 🍃

One evening when I was twenty-five years old, my then husband went out to study with some friends. He was in college after having returned from Iraq and using the GI Bill to try to do something with his life. I was holding down the fort by being the breadwinner, taking care of his seven-year-old son, and being the wife and mom and housekeeper and cook. You know, all that stuff. And that night he just didn't come home.

I'd tried to call him over the course of a couple of hours, but his phone gradually went from no answer to no ringing at all. I drove out in the darkness to search for him with my sleeping stepson in tow. Ultimately, I found neither his car nor his body and I came home in tears. When he finally materialized in the early morning hours, he unceremoniously told me that he'd been with someone else and didn't want to be married to me anymore. He grabbed a change of clothes, left to stay in a hotel, and I cried my eyes out on the floor of my closet until the sun started to rise. In a single evening, I'd witnessed the end of a nearly nine-year relationship for reasons I still don't understand.

In the months afterward, I floated untethered because I was alone for the first time in my adult life. I had no sense of who I was or what my new life was supposed to be. I was twenty-six years old and struggling to cope, so one day I decided to pick up my first beer. You know, to do that super unhealthy coping thing adults like to do all the time. Alcohol was a prime (and legal) choice. Eventually I moved on to wine and later to vodka, because these didn't turn my stomach like the beer did and worked much better anyway.

I began running too. Not literally running, but I was never in one place for very long because I simply couldn't bear to be. And as the next few years rolled by, I found that my need to run, to drown feelings, to flee ... it stayed with me. Eventually I popped open a bottle of wine and drank a glass or two every night. I took dance classes after work so I wouldn't have to go home. I spent my weekends in clubs, ordering rum and

Cokes and chasing them down with a Smirnoff Ice or two. Then I'd kiss random people in dark corners in an attempt to dull the loneliness, before stumbling out the door and making my way home in the wee hours.

I couldn't sleep, I couldn't eat. I felt like I walked through my days in a dream state, sometimes not even really feeling human. I'd lost three clothing sizes and people started telling me I looked sick. But what they didn't know was that every time I tried to eat, the nausea overwhelmed me to a point where starvation was more pleasant. So I started buying milkshakes and French fries just to get some calories into my body.

I remember very clearly thinking to myself, *I'm going to get sick.* As the months and years marched on, my thoughts got more specific. *I hope I don't get cancer.* I was young (late twenties), still very naïve, and yet I knew I was draining the life from my body. I knew I was going to break but I just didn't know when. So I crossed my fingers and kept going, doing the very best I could.

But the problem is, stress is cumulative. Life is cumulative. You can't keep taking away from the balance and then expecting to come out okay on the other side. The people who believe you can are the people who turn into the sad stories of life. The ones who have regrets, the ones who wish they'd done things differently, the ones whose world comes crashing down when their bodies finally decide to give out.

I coasted along for about nine years after that, coming down with quite a few colds and several bouts of pneumonia, but never (thank goodness) being diagnosed with anything scarier than that. I began to think that maybe I had an extra tough body, that maybe it could take much more than I had given it credit for. I'm sure a lot of us think we can handle much more than we actually can.

But what I learned is that we're okay until we're not. People do not suddenly have heart attacks, or suddenly get cancer, or suddenly have an autoimmune disease. They may appear as sudden occurrences, but in reality, those health issues have been gaining momentum—unchecked—for a long period of time. Then they manifest when life has gone past a point of no return. And it may be your fault (i.e., you're a workaholic-alcoholic who doesn't sleep) or it may just be the way things are (you have crappy genes or are simply unlucky).

Me? I suddenly was not okay. Like—*wham!*—not okay.

It started with surgery to remove fibroids that had suddenly blown up to grapefruit size (I believe the death of my cat sent my health over the edge). A week later, my surgeon sent me to the ER and we found out my gallbladder had decided it was done playing. I had another major surgery less than six weeks after that. I thought I'd finally be done and on my way, but as I said earlier, stress is cumulative. The body piles emotions and stress on top of emotions and other stress. Injury on top of injury. These two events ended up being the start of my chronic illness journey; a journey I'm still surprised to be on considering I was never predisposed to illness on the whole. But it's also a journey that makes perfect sense considering all the stress, heartache, abuse, and other issues I'd dealt with before age thirty.

By that point, I'd been through a tough childhood, financial difficulties, a war, infidelity, divorce, long-term unemployment, and the loss of a child.

I've spent a lot of time since those surgeries thinking about how you don't see illness coming ... and yet you do. About how even though you know you're putting unreasonable amounts of stress on your body, you either can't change it or you don't want to. Maybe your destructive behavior soothes you in the moment (denial is a great coping mechanism). Maybe it quells something else you don't want to face, like a fear of death or a fear of failure. Maybe you pop a bottle of wine every night or eat a big brownie because you're searching for something you don't feel inside, or maybe you're trying to dull something you do feel. Maybe you can't relax on vacation and instead answer your emails because you just can't be alone with yourself, even when there's a beautiful vista ahead or you get the opportunity to spend extra time with your spouse. In all of this, you still believe you'll be fine because nothing has happened yet.

We must realize that our bodies are not indestructible machines, and we should live every day with an awareness of *how* we are living that day. Ask yourself: am I adding to my life's balance or taking something away? Have I rested today? Have I done something that makes me happy? Have I practiced good self-care by eating nutritious food and taking a walk in the breeze? Or am I falling face-first into bed at midnight, a ragged mess, after a stressful day at work that I doused in two margaritas at happy hour?

❧ ❧ ❧

Being healthy is a blessing and not a given. Ultimately, it's temporary too. We're all going to die. And we die because our bodies decide they're tired of chugging along, or because something on the other side of the sky has decided our time here is up. Making the best of your life is much easier when you have your health. You can still have a meaningful, wonderful life if you struggle with illness, but why choose a path toward illness when you still have quite a bit of power to choose a path toward health?

We all have a choice. I've been working for several years now on finding my way to remission after all of the running in my twenties. I've learned that it's much easier to stay in a healthy place than to try to crawl your way back when you've lost your way. Luckily for me, it doesn't seem to be too late just yet. Although it really almost was.

Listen to your body, take care of yourself, and don't wait until it's too late.

LIFE SHOWS YOU
YOUR CALLING

Finding a calling or purpose (or in some circles "dharma") is a struggle many of us wrestle with on a daily basis. It's certainly been something I've actively fretted over for a large part of my adult life.

I first knew there was a serious problem when I hit my junior year of college. I ran out of general education classes, hadn't selected a major (and didn't have any inclination toward one), so I took an entire semester of random courses simply to try to figure it out. I enrolled in art history, sociology, technical theatre, environmental science, and a career planning class. Each of these subjects was interesting, but "interesting" does not a major make.

The career planning class was the one I put a lot of energy into, because it was supposed to help me find some sense of direction. I remember slogging through test after test to try to create labels for my personality and inclinations. We took the MAPP test, which was probably one of the most insightful assessments, as well as a number of other personality and aptitude tests. Then we spent the remainder of our class time talking through the results and about different career paths. I remember feeling like I still had no sense of direction despite all of that chatter and analysis. In fact, I'll never forget the day one of my tests said that my number one career path was as a mortician. I was horrified that something about my answers matched me up to a career working with the dead. Clearly these tests couldn't tell me the things I really needed to know.

I ended up becoming an English major in the eleventh hour, and I had some very logical reasons for doing so that had nothing to do with hopes and dreams. First, I liked reading stories and learning about people. Second, I figured I would much rather read stories than textbooks if I were going to have to do so for a few years. And third, my eleventh grade English teacher had told me I was a strong writer, so I figured I'd go where my talent supposedly was. The decision felt good and I never regretted it, so for that moment in time I felt like I was going in the right direction.

But when I graduated with my plain ol' bachelor of arts degree in English, I found myself parked on a dark road that I had thought I'd be driving down in the sunshine. I hadn't planned to be a teacher, so I didn't get the certification. In fact, I hadn't planned anything at all and was just hoping to be shown some sort of direction when I got there. After I walked across that stage and moved back home to Texas, I found myself with no concrete career plan as I stepped timidly into my first years of true adulthood. Things were challenging for a long while.

I honestly never thought I would become a writer of *any* kind—not when I was growing up, not when I was an English major, and not even in those early years of my career when I was struggling to put food on the table and keep a roof over my head as a technical writer. I used to bemoan how much I disliked it, mostly because I was writing about computer software and that was the least important thing on my radar. But I look back with my hindsight goggles and I see the universe had me there so I could practice the craft. I would not have had the motivation to write anything on my own at that time in my life; I just had too many obligations and too much stress. So those jobs that I felt like were all wrong for me actually were helping me hone my skills. *Something* knew more than I did about what was to eventually come.

☙ ☙ ☙

When I reached my late twenties and my life imploded, I expended enormous amounts of effort repeating those same career tests, thinking about what I was good at, trying to understand what kind of options I might have, and reaching for some sort of direction about where I was to go. I had gotten divorced due to my partner's infidelity, I'd lost everything I had (including my home, twice, thanks to the marital split and later to the economic crisis), and I now had to rebuild a new life on my own with a future that was no longer written in the way I'd expected it to be. I'd even lost my technical writing job and couldn't get another one because of the Great Recession. I couldn't get a job as a copywriter either. So I assumed I was completely off course and needed to redirect myself. *Clearly,* I said to myself, *I've been lost all along or things would have turned out better.*

Sometimes life surprises you with your calling. Sometimes you fall into it even though you've been trying to avoid it, and sometimes you don't see it coming at all. Maybe you're fumbling around in the dark and a light appears in the distance, so you start walking in that direction just to get away from where you are.

While I stumbled around, grasping at air and trying my hand at different jobs, I wrote in my journals and in a blog—for what ended up being about nine years. I say I wrote, but I more vomited onto the page anything and everything that was bothering me. I considered this vomiting to be something anyone might do to work through their crap—not something a writer might do—so I didn't pay much attention to it. People often ignore these small clues in their lives.

The first time I even recall thinking I might like to be a writer was when I started trying to pen the story of my first marriage. It was a sad, war-torn experience that went down in flames, but I thought it might make a good story (or at the very least get it out of my system). I never finished that book ... or the next book ... or the one after that. And this is because right about the time I was finally building momentum and thinking I was getting somewhere, I got sick. Really sick. Like, *I almost didn't exist anymore* sick. I mentioned earlier in the book that I had two surgeries to remove the fibroids and my broken gallbladder, but what I didn't mention was that by the time I rolled up to the hospital for the second time (crying heavily in the passenger seat, mind you, because I couldn't believe I was about to be cut open again), my obstructed gallbladder had inflamed my pancreas so badly that it could have been the end of me in a different time period. Thank you, modern medicine. I was down for the count for a few years after that.

As you might imagine, being sick was like stomping the brakes on my life again—on my motivation, on everything. I was finally diagnosed with mast cell disease during this time, which would become my most debilitating diagnosis and one that I still struggle to manage today. It prevented me from working (and writing) as much as I would have liked. I did try to pen another novel during that time in an effort to not waste my life any further, but I crashed and burned harder on that novel than on any before it. I imploded so badly, in fact, that I would just stare helplessly at my screen as my fingers stood still—completely out of ideas, out of words, out of spark.

Clearly I was wasting my time. Clearly this was not meant to be.

I then abandoned writing entirely for a year—a whole year—until one day, almost as if being pushed by something outside of me, I trudged back and sat down at my computer.

Maybe everything that happened in my life needed to happen in the order it did, just like maybe everything that's happened in your life needed to happen. Maybe your "thing" will come when it's time, like a river rushes down a mountain only when the spring comes to melt the snow. One of the biggest lessons I've learned from being sick and almost signing off of planet Earth is: you've got to let things flow. Stop fighting, just ride along.

This book came from the sum of all my life experiences thus far. And when I look at my journey, I can see that my calling was there all along but was waiting for the right time to emerge. I can't write fiction very well because perhaps that's not what I'm supposed to do (yet). I thought I couldn't pursue nonfiction because I'd told myself it wasn't "real" writing and therefore wasn't a valid purpose anyway. In my mind, my purpose had to be something real. It had to be something that was less silly than sitting here writing about my life.

But I've learned we all have a purpose that may seem trivial to us, but actually is not trivial at all. Some people would say what I'm doing now is ridiculous. Who cares about my life and what I've learned? But then a few people might care, and if they do, then what I did meant something to the world because it meant something to some of the people in it.

The same logic applies if you're a lawn guy, where you trudge in every day not understanding why your lot in life is to mow lawns. But you know what? Someone is happy to see that lawn looking beautiful. An elderly woman who cannot take care of her landscaping is thrilled to be helped by you. A single mother who was abandoned by her partner has one less thing to worry about because you took care of the lawn. You see what I mean?

Life will show you what you're meant to do, you just have to pay attention and have some patience. My life trained me for about four decades to do what I'm doing now. It filled my head with experiences, wisdom, life. It made sure my skills stayed sharp by placing me in jobs that required me to write and to practice my craft, even when I hated the jobs and felt like I was squandering the days I was given. Most recently, it moved me into a life position of greater financial security and time flexibility, which then allowed me to sit down and do this thing I'm doing without the pressures I used to have on a daily basis.

␪ ␪ ␪

Give life credit and allow it to show you what you're supposed to do. Flow along a little bit. See where the road takes you. When you get there, you'll bop yourself on the head because it will all seem *so* stupidly obvious. But that's okay.

I think some people know what they want to do when they are ten years old and are prepared to do that thing. Others have a journey to take before they can do the thing they're supposed to do, so they don't understand it until later. If you don't know what your purpose is yet, take heart. You are already living it. You are already on the journey you are supposed to take. Your purpose exists, whether you can see and verbalize it yet or not.

TO WALLOW IS HUMAN

I'm one of those people who struggles with depression to varying degrees. I don't know if it's truly a chemical thing or if it's a result of the challenging life I led during my first thirty years. But I know I struggle with prolonged feelings of inertia and sadness, and some days I just don't want to try anymore.

And by "try," I mean some days I don't want to do life. I don't want to do my work, I don't want to write my books, I don't want to read or watch TV. Some days, the only things I can make myself do are things that take me somewhere outside of myself and my own survival. Things like feeding my elderly cat, or helping out a neighbor, or sending a charitable contribution to those in need after a disaster.

I used to think some people in life had it easy and some people were stuck in constant train wrecks. I still have these thoughts when I get into the bad habit of comparing myself to others, but I also now realize most people struggle with various things at various times, and they sometimes wallow as part of that process. If they didn't, there would be no suicide, no drug abuse, no family feuds, no broken friendships.

I first really came to this understanding when I went on a solo trip to Hawaii at age thirty. I was beyond burned out after spending a year of my life teaching in a public school and being berated by a principal who was hurling personal anger in my direction. I'd also gotten notice of a layoff about six weeks prior, which was mandated for all first-year teachers in the state due to budget cuts, so I'd been feverishly job searching in my spare moments in the hopes of being rescued. While I loved my kids and loved showing them how to read and write, the ongoing demands of the job had far surpassed what I could absorb. I'd also struggled to speak Spanish every day to help the fifth-graders who still needed language support, as I was barely fluent myself. I'd been falling into a hole and wallowing in sadness since about October.

I'd interviewed at a corporation shortly after the layoff announcement. It gave me really bad vibes, but they called and offered me a position as a technical writer one April afternoon and I needed a job desperately by that point. School would be over in a month, I was single, and I had no other income to rely on but my own. I remember standing very still in the middle of my classroom after hanging up the phone, feeling a polarity of sensations churning inside of me. I felt relief because I'd averted financial disaster and now had a plan, but I also felt a pronounced dread about the new position. I'd sat at a long and empty conference room table during my interview, looking into the faces of people who didn't smile much and who struggled to ask me any real questions. Something just wasn't right and I knew it from that moment, but what other option did I have?

I looked up at the big clock above my classroom door as I often did all day long: it was 3:35 p.m. and I was free to leave any time after 3:30, per faculty rules. My eyes moved from there and scanned my classroom in a panoramic sort of way, looking at all of the details. The books on the shelf that I'd bought my students for reading time. The computers along the wall. The files on my desk. The big cabinet in the corner. The desks I'd set in groups of four, again per faculty rules. I let it all imprint itself on my brain and I took a deep breath, and then I gathered my purse and my water bottle, and I walked out.

I didn't consciously know that I wouldn't ever return, but I suppose my insides had a hunch because there was a finality to it that felt like wind going out of my sails. I buzzed my badge at the side exit and moved across the schoolyard to the parking lot, feeling the warmth of the afternoon sunlight on my skin. I got into my car, drove across town to my one bedroom apartment, and spent an hour or two with the covers over my head before eventually drifting off to sleep.

I slept for three days. Literally. I was the most tired I've ever been. I only got up to eat and to send an email to my principal saying that I was not coming back, and to please give the kids my love. If this is what it feels like to almost work yourself to death, I think I now have a good understanding.

I rubbed my eyes a few days later and finally changed out of my pajamas, ready to take stock of my life and what was coming next. On a whim, I decided to use all of my credit card miles to book a solo trip. I'm not sure what made me look up Hawaii aside from it being a beach, but it turned out I had enough airline miles to go for free. For FREE! All I'd have to do was find a hotel and scrimp together some food. It was now or never, so I decided to make it now.

During that trip, I met all sorts of people. I met a track runner from Louisiana who I hung out with on the beach two or three times. I met a coach from Mississippi who was there with a bunch of high school kids, and with whom I shared sushi and a big piece of cake. I met a lovely man from Sweden who was doing an around-the-world trek all by himself, and he was finishing up one of the last legs of his journey. And then I met a divorced middle-aged gentleman from San Diego who loved to surf, who came to Hawaii often, and who had a story to tell.

The gentleman and I met for breakfast every morning at a café right on the beach that was a good twenty-minute trek from my hotel. We'd talk about life and sorrows and dreams and goals. He told me about the failure of his marriage and the pain he still harbored, and how he used surfing as a distraction every day after work so he could lose himself in the waves. And it was then I realized, for the first time, that I did not have the monopoly on sorrow—nor was I the only person who wallowed in it sometimes.

Most people have sorrows, it turns out, and some of them are just as deep as mine. It was eye-opening and life-changing to hear someone much older than me share his ongoing pain so openly. And the experience freed me up to wallow without sinking. To feel without drowning. To pull myself back up so I could keep going through life. I no longer felt so isolated in my feelings and I began to understand that tough times are just part of the human condition. All of these realizations are helpful for your logical brain when your emotional one is running away with itself, and mine was at that time in my life. Sometimes you need your logical brain to re-engage so you don't lose yourself in the swirl indefinitely.

I returned from that trip refreshed and ready to continue past any lingering sadness over my teaching experience. I was still lonely, I was still dreading my new job, and I still felt mildly cursed. But I was able to put things into perspective and move forward to my next chapter.

That job did turn out to be one of the worst corporate jobs of my career, but I was able to get through it and keep going. Remembering my friend from Hawaii who also had sorrows, I'd let myself scream and cry in my car and then I'd march back into my new office, sit in my gray cubicle, and keep trying to shape the experience into something else.

🍃 🍃 🍃

I share this story to say that I think it's okay to feel your sadness for a while, even to the point of wallowing. After many years of telling myself I should get over it ("it" being whatever is bothering me, or "it" being nothing actually identifiable in the moment), or that

I should not devote energy to staring at the wall or pulling the covers up over my face in the middle of the afternoon. I finally made a new rule for myself: it's okay to feel my feelings and to sink into them, as long as I pick myself up eventually and crawl out of the hole. Because this is something everyone does in order to make it through life.

So, wallow if you need to. But find whatever it is that snaps you out of it so you don't sink to the bottom. Maybe it's a brownie. Maybe it's a solo trip to Hawaii. Maybe it's volunteering for a cause greater than yourself. Whatever you do, pick yourself up and keep going—and realize you are one of billions of people who have a need to wallow sometimes in order to process and move past feelings. Good will come, bad will come. People will be wonderful, people will suck. The secret is learning how to overcome whatever it is, understanding that it's just a part of life, and continuing to push toward your next adventure.

SOME PEOPLE
HATE BOUNDARIES

*S*o you've decided you're fed up with someone or something. A part of your life just isn't working for you. Maybe your mother-in-law won't stop showing up at odd hours at your front door. Maybe your boss acts like everything is on fire and always comes to you at the eleventh hour. Maybe your neighbor is blaring music at 11:00 p.m. and the thumping keeps you awake and pissed off every night. Or maybe (and this happens a lot, it has happened to me in the past although thankfully not in the present) your partner is treating you less than ideally. You'd like him or her to treat you differently, but you haven't figured out how to speak up because you're afraid of the backlash.

Most of us have a breaking point where we decide we can't tolerate things anymore. Getting to that point is different for everyone, though. If you have a healthy sense of self and are confident in who you are, you'll probably reach yours fairly quickly—long before the situation escalates to utter despair or fuming rage. If you are less sure of yourself, if you're shy, or if you're codependent and worry more about other people's feelings than you do your own, getting to a place where you finally set a boundary will be more slow to come.

I realized in my late twenties that I was a total codependent pushover and hadn't even noticed. I took on everyone else's feelings and made them my own, and in fact made them even more important than my own. I went even further by meshing my personality with other people's such that I didn't know who I was anymore. My goal in life was to do anything I could to make those around me happy.

My codependency was noble and honorable to an extent. I mean, many of us do want to help others and be good to those around us, especially when it comes to the people we love. But it's no longer noble or honorable when that behavior starts damaging you on the inside. And this is why boundaries are part of the human experience, and why I had to learn how to set them in order to leave those behaviors behind as I moved into my thirties.

The hardest part about boundaries is people often don't respond to them in the ways we might wish or expect them to. And these can be people we love or people we really, really dislike. There are several instances in my life where setting a boundary caused people to disappear completely, to come at me with rage, to fire me, to ignore me, or even to spew venom publicly about who I was as a person. The different reactions you may experience when you set a boundary are enormous in quantity and intensity, and what you get depends on the health of the person being subjected to the boundary.

☙ ☙ ☙

When I was twenty-three years old, I finally got the courage to stand up to my mother and set some boundaries. It was Mother's Day and we were in another tug-of-war about how she felt I needed to do more for her, and how I felt I needed space to manage my own life. The fight escalated to a discussion of the past, where I started pulling out incidences from my childhood that had wounded me and that I'd never dared to talk to her about. She responded by turning the tables and accusing me of doing an equal amount of wrongs to *her*, all the way back to when I was a toddler.

I then told my mother I would not allow her to continue to berate me about things I had done to her when I was five years old. Things I couldn't remember and that I should not be blamed for. I also strongly disagreed with her assessment that I had ruined her life. She didn't like my unwillingness to accept her perspective, but I set the boundary anyway and I held firm. When she refused to respect the boundary, insisting I must listen to what she wanted to say about all the things I did to her as a child, I told her I loved her and I left. When I called her the next day, she hung up on me.

We haven't spoken since.

I also experienced boundary difficulties more than once during my corporate career. In one instance, I'd been working in my field for a while and was trying to get somewhere better than where I'd landed, but the opportunities were just not coming. I was being pushed down, promises were being broken, new challenges were being given away, and promotions were being handed to others (to men, but that's another problem). One day I got tired of it and scheduled a meeting with the head of the department. I asked him if I could at least be an equal rather than the lowest person on the totem pole; I was managing myself, doing equal work, and had proven myself over time. Hell, I didn't even need a pay raise, I just wanted to be *equal*.

A few months later I was unceremoniously fired without cause, and was told "it just isn't working out." I was escorted out of the building like a criminal and I sat on the curb behind the back entrance, crying with my head in my hands, wondering what the hell I was going to do now.

※ ※ ※

Boundaries can be hard for some of us to set, especially when others' reactions are like those I described. I'm only now learning how to put those boundaries into place before total resentment or seething anger sets in on my part, and this is probably because doing so doesn't always fix things. In fact, setting boundaries can make the situation feel so much worse because some people are really good at making you believe the problem is you. Like you're the oddball, like you're the one who isn't seeing the world in the correct way, like you're the one who is being unreasonable. I've learned this type of reaction is just a part of the push and pull of relationships. It's part of people's own defensiveness or unhealthy tendencies they might project onto you, because sometimes it's too hard for them to actually look at how they are treating others.

And you know what else? If I set a reasonable boundary and you balk, I probably don't need you in my life anyway. Separating yourself is obviously harder when you're dealing with people who won't go away (or people you can't get away from), like your boss or your brother-in-law. But you just have to learn to navigate, to set your boundaries in the best way you can, to learn what sets other people off and what doesn't, and to play to their best emotions when you're trying to get your point across.

🍃 🍃 🍃

My two rules of boundaries now are as follows. First: set them, dammit! Stop letting yourself be taken through months (or years) of turbulence before you finally open your mouth. Second: know there may be negative consequences. Be prepared, and be okay with that.

We all need to live our lives in a way that makes sure *we* are treated with kindness while we simultaneously treat others in that manner. Sometimes self-protection is necessary, though, because not everyone we interact with has that same approach to life. They will stomp on you if you allow it. So make sure to put up those gates (or cement walls) when you've finally had enough. And maybe practice not waiting until you've finally had enough; maybe do it when you're halfway to finally having enough.

And also? Love yourself more. Stand up for yourself more. But always do it with kindness, with tact, and with skill (you'll need this for some especially challenging homo sapiens). If it doesn't come naturally to you now, it will in time. Everything takes practice to get it right.

YOUR
"MEANINGLESS" JOB

*W*hen I was fifteen years old, I tried desperately to secure a job as a carhop at the local Sonic drive-in. I'd heard through the grapevine (and obviously through an unreliable one) that they would hire girls my age—a full year younger than the legal working age in Texas. I should have known that laws are *actually* laws, but I was young and stubborn and wanted to generate income for myself. I needed things as a young high school student—like clothes and makeup and toiletries—that my mother was too poor to provide for me at the time.

When I chose Sonic as my target employer, I wasn't thinking about the significance of my job as a carhop or whether it was changing the world. I was just thinking about it being the only pathway to money at age fifteen. I tried in vain for a week or two (a long time in teenage years) before giving up and biding my time until my sixteenth birthday, after which I swiftly got a job at a local movie theater in the concession stand. I made

$4.25 per hour and, like most teenagers, I didn't think about my work beyond the paycheck.

I ended up working a myriad of jobs between the ages of sixteen and twenty-three that were just a paycheck and nothing more. I'd worked in the concession stand only a few months before moving on to a job in the photo lab at the local drugstore. I did this for almost two years before trying my hand at waiting tables at a regional Tex-Mex chain, because I was eighteen now and old enough to serve alcohol. I'd assumed waitressing would be a greener (financially speaking) pasture for my last semester of high school, but I turned out to be an appalling server, dropping salsa on a newborn baby one day and spilling an entire tray of water on a woman in a business suit on another. I quit after two months, finished out my senior year, and jumped ship to a dorm room an hour north of my hometown. I studied there just one academic year before transferring out to another state to get even further away.

I worked a number of part-time jobs during my college years but still didn't philosophize about them; they were simply a means to put food in my mouth, to pay the rent on my tiny apartment across from the Kraft cheese factory, and to replace my tire when I ran over a nail. If campus jobs were available, that was great and I took them. But they were a rare occurrence, so I had to find other ways to get by.

Mostly I found myself working a variety of retail jobs and even at Chuck E. Cheese. Toward the end of my college years, I'd started feeling like my jobs were sucking some of the light out of my soul. But I reminded myself that someday I wouldn't be unclogging toilets and cleaning up children's vomit. Someday I wouldn't be standing in a desert-quiet retail store at dinner time, shuffling back and forth in my khaki pants to transfer weight between my aching feet.

Someday, I'd think, *I'll have a better job.*

I had many of these silent conversations with myself during that time in my working life, and they controlled any runaway frustrations for the most part because I knew I still had a promising future on the other side of my college diploma. Through these little pep talks, I was able to keep my determination strong and my spirits high even on the worst of my working days. It wasn't until I got out of college and experienced the eight-to-five pace of corporate America that I began to believe I was missing something.

🍃 🍃 🍃

I'd landed in a bland cubicle with gray walls, grasping helplessly at IT speak I couldn't understand. And when I wasn't attempting translation, I was staring blankly at a computer screen for so long that I got daily headaches—all the while struggling to pay my bills on a temp worker salary.

I remember one instance when I gathered with coworkers around a large table in a conference room, surrounded by walls of glass and random employees walking by, and I thought to myself, *I don't care about any of this. Where are the lively discussions about things that matter, like I had in my lit classes? How did I get here? I'm so bored and unhappy.*

I'd arrived in *the* place (corporate America), the final destination after college and for the rest of my life, and it was absolutely not what I'd pep-talked myself into during those retail years. In fact, I felt more miserable than I ever had during my college jobs because I now spent my entire life chained to a desk. I also had no hope for a future that might look any different because this, I believed, is what people did when they got their degrees.

I've spent a good portion of the last fifteen years trying to figure out how my job matters and, honestly, if it does at all. I think a lot of us do this as we try to search for meaning in our lives and whatever that "thing" is that we're supposed to do while we're here. We either feel like we haven't found our calling yet, which is distressing on many levels, or we feel like what we're currently doing simply doesn't matter at all—not to the bugs on the wall, or to the wind in the trees, or to the bosses behind glass office windows.

I worked those corporate jobs for a long time and was convinced that my life was a waste, that somehow I'd squandered the opportunity to be whomever I was truly supposed to be, simply because the life map I was holding wasn't showing me any other way. During my quiet moments, in between staring listlessly at the computer screen or trudging through tasks I didn't care about, I often studied the older people around me to get a gauge on their happiness levels. Were they feeling what I felt? Or was I an enigma?

❧ ❧ ❧

At that first job in the gray cubicle, my desk was right by the stairwell and very close to the elevators, so it was easy to catch passing conversations or to observe behavior without being noticed. And what I saw was how some people seemed content while others projected misery. I wasn't exactly sure what to make of it all until I focused on the custodial staff going in and out with their brooms and buckets. Over time they began to stop and say "hello," because I spoke a little Spanish. They were friendly, happy, and sometimes actually whistled while they worked. I enjoyed talking to them because it allowed me to practice a different language, and they enjoyed talking to me because very few of the other white-collar workers would even say "good afternoon."

Unlike me, these staff members didn't seem to think their lives were a waste. Maybe they weren't doing exactly what they wanted to be doing, but they had jobs and they were making money for their families. They could at least work in a respectable establishment where they didn't have to fear for their safety or be subjected to unchecked abuse from those around them. And as I got older and learned more about working and careers and the world, I came to understand that *everyone's* job matters. No job is truly meaningless, even if we don't find meaning in it ourselves.

Those custodial workers kept the bathrooms clean so I could feel more comfortable using them. They kept the paper towels stocked, the wastepaper baskets emptied, and the building functioning like a well-oiled machine. This was useful not only to me but to thirteen floors of other humans who trudged in every day. And I, in turn, (even though I felt utterly defeated some days) was contributing to the company and to my boss in some way. I was talking to people and having a positive impact on their days. I was making a bit of money for my family, and I was gaining skills that would allow me to eventually get a better job.

Everything had a purpose. My job, their job, the jobs of others around me.

☙ ☙ ☙

Maybe you're not supposed to be Jennifer Aniston or Steve Jobs, and maybe you're not supposed to be the CEO in the corner office. Maybe you're not supposed to be the coffee shop owner, or the lawyer defending the persecuted. Maybe your life is supposed to be more simple or self-contained. So maybe it's okay if you're an administrative assistant, or a janitor, or a temp worker. Maybe it's okay if you're just doing a job that fills a need in the world (like answering the phone with a cheerful "hello"), that takes care of you or your family or your dogs, and that gives you something to do every day so you don't wallow in depression and subsequently end up under a bridge.

I'm not saying every job situation is sublime and without reproach. There are shitty jobs out there and shitty employers and shitty pay, and we all need to get out of those situations if we are able to do so. But what I *am* saying is that no matter what job you do—even if you don't feel like it matters to you personally or isn't accomplishing some sort of lofty goal—your job matters. Even if it's not the job you do forever or the one you truly want to be doing, it *matters*. Every job is important. Just like every human is important.

🍂 🍂 🍂

Finally recognizing my job's significance helped me find more contentment, as I moved forward in my life, with whatever work came my way. I'd decided sitting in a gray cubicle every day was crushing my soul, so I got out of that. I don't always get to do the work I want to do or the work I feel I have the talent to do, but I somehow always get *some* work just in time. And this work allows me to pay my bills, and travel a little bit, and take care of my health, and feed my two rescue cats. It allows me to live in a place I can call home, even if I don't own it. It provides me with new skills, even if they aren't the skills I was going after in the first place. It allows me to contribute something to the world where I otherwise might not have contributed anything.

The turning point for me was sitting down and thinking about all the people my work impacted in a day or week or month. As one example, the work I did at a certain time in my life allowed construction guys to have a job to take care of their families. It allowed their company to have a website that would help them gain more business, which would in turn help everyone employed there. My job also took some of the burden, stress, and work off of another employee, who could assign me tasks when she was overloaded—even if those tasks were not all that interesting or meaningful (and they often weren't). The point is, I found tangible ways in which my "meaningless" work was more meaningful, and I think that's the key to finding contentment.

These days I still strive to learn and to grow in my career. I still strive for certain types of work, and of course for work like I'm doing as I write this book, but I also feel much more at peace with whatever my life is. I no longer fight the job, saying it's not what I want or not what I should be doing. It *is* what I should be doing, because I'm doing it! I wouldn't be doing it if it weren't what I was supposed to be doing.

Say that a few times out loud.

FINDING CONFIDENCE WHEN YOUR LIFE HISTORY IS CONTRADICTIVE

I wasn't one of those kids who was constantly put on a pedestal, encouraged by the idea that I could be whomever I wanted to be or that I was "enough" just the way I was. I wasn't really told I was smart, talented, or pretty. Instead, I grew up in a home where nothing I did was ever right (at least, according to my mother). I was perpetually grounded, I was yelled at in dramatic fashion for the smallest of transgressions, and when I lacked confidence in both my appearance and in my shy personality as I moved into middle and high school, there was nobody to build up what was shattering inside of me. This lack of validation can be devastating for a child and doesn't automatically "right" itself when that child becomes an adult.

🍂 🍂 🍂

I think a person's sense of self has to come from somewhere outside of their own brain as they're becoming aware of who they are and how they exist in the world. Someone has to tell you you're okay, or you're more than okay, otherwise you can spend your entire adolescence believing you're a giant flaw. This belief can translate to feelings of not measuring up to the kids in school, or to thinking you're not as "good" as your sibling in the adjacent bedroom, or to feeling "less than" whomever else you decide to latch on to and emulate as the ideal of what you should be.

My own feelings of inadequacy carried into adulthood; I simply didn't have the right tools to overcome them on my own for a while, and didn't even know where to start. I did get some sense of self from my grandmother as a young adult, because she thought I was the bees knees and often told me so. But since she was just one person, and because my mother didn't seem to share the same sentiment, her loving words weren't enough to counter the negative thoughts that had gathered strength over the last couple of decades. And this is probably why I got married at twenty-one, chasing the high school boyfriend who gave me the only sense of self I'd ever had.

I thought I was happy in that marriage for several years. In hindsight, it was probably because he gave me so much of what I hadn't received (and had needed) as a child or young adult. It wasn't because we were such a great match and therefore should embark on a life together; it was more that we needed each other to help fill the voids we both had in the pits of our souls due to our childhoods (his was spent in foster care). I felt like I could believe him when he said I was loveable and good enough, because he knew me inside and out and had chosen to marry me anyway. I'm sure he felt the same way about me on some level too.

During that marriage, I coasted along with a shaky (but improved) sense of self that somehow got me through the tough times. But after our marriage ended, all of his assurances and promises dissolved into dust. If I truly *were* all of the things he'd built me up to be, why did he leave? In my mind it was now decidedly true that I was, as I had always suspected, unworthy and broken. Any sense of confidence I'd developed must have been an illusion I'd wrapped around myself for the past eight-and-a-half years (we'd been together since I was seventeen). My mother was right all along; I wasn't good enough.

I was in my mid-twenties when he left. Since I no longer had any sort of parental figure around most of the time, and I'd just lost my beloved grandmother a few months prior, I regressed to the feelings of inadequacy I'd felt as a child. And, wow, was I lost. I distinctly remember detaching from reality some days, my mind floating in the ether without enough sense of self to even hold me to the ground. I didn't know who I was or what I liked or what I wanted, much less whether any of those things would be good enough once I figured it all out. This was one of the harder times of my life.

᷍ ᷍ ᷍

By the time my current husband and I started dating about five years later, I was flopping around like a fish. I'd just come out of an abusive relationship that had set me back so far, I was sticking notes on my bathroom mirror to try to rebuild my self-esteem. That man had not only verbally and emotionally abused me, he'd also pinned me down and tried to punch me in the face. I was truly at one of the lowest confidence points I'd been in since my adolescence.

As I got older, and as I spent more years with my second husband, I learned that you can discover confidence even if you haven't had it historically. And I'm not going to say you can easily find it within yourself, because I couldn't. Before he came along, I dated many people who had to regularly offer me the outside reassurance I still needed, yet I couldn't seem to find a sustainable sense of self—even with the encouragement. As things got more serious, I struggled heavily with the idea that I would be worth marrying and staying married to. Would he leave me just like the last one left, due to some reason tied to a flaw within myself that I still hadn't figured out?

Over time these fears began to quiet, because my husband was not the only person who tried to help me feel okay with *me*. I had friends who'd encouraged me for many years, primarily by listening to my fears and offering verbal support, plus one or two good guys whom I'd dated amongst the bad. What my husband does now to encourage me is sort of a continuation of that.

Although at the same time, he can't spend too much of his time building me up, because who wants to spend their entire life trying to make someone who doesn't feel worthy of herself feel like she is? Nobody wants to do that. It's a poor use of time. So I do my own confidence building these days. And I've done it by building on the words of the people currently in my world and of those still living in my memory. I pull confidence from those years when people told me I was a good person who was enough, and from the knowledge that my husband loves me and wanted to marry me. He wanted to spend the rest of his life with nobody else but me—despite all of my issues and baggage. I continue to build on these reassurances in order to create a new feeling of confidence I never had in the first decades of my life.

🖉 🖉 🖉

I think there are extraordinary people in the world who have unshakeable senses of self. My husband is one of those people, and his self-assurance is quite amazing to me when I contrast it to myself. But I also think people like him must have grown up in environments that cultivated those feelings—ones that nurtured and grew their confidence into mature oak trees, or into giant redwoods, such that they could stand tall against anything without so much as losing a piece of bark.

Since I'm not one of those people, and I would venture to guess a large portion of society does not have the luxury of a fully supported childhood either, I offer this advice: focus on those who believe in you when you don't believe in yourself. Most people have at least one person who does, whether it's a coworker or an aunt or a neighbor. Most people have one person on planet Earth who sees them for who they are and loves them anyway.

Because let's face it, unless you're an axe murderer or a money launderer, you're probably okay. And you should, therefore, be confident in who you are and what you have to offer. Maybe you don't have the best legs, but maybe you have the most beautiful eyes. Maybe you're not good at checking off your "To Do" list, but maybe you're a badass creative force who has amazing ideas. Focus on the good. Grow your own confidence until maybe it's not the size of a thousand-year-old oak tree or a giant redwood, but until it's strong enough to withstand the storms of life. Until it can bend and twist and not break.

Even the smallest trees can do this, you know.

STEP AWAY FROM
THE SCREEN

*I*t seems like there is this constant buzzing with all
the technology around us—and not a good sort
of buzzing like a bumble bee that pollinates the
tomatoes I'm going to eat next month. It's a buzzing
like my brain is on speed and I can't get away. Or like
I'm on a stationary bike in the world's longest spin class,
and I'm going to eventually spin myself completely off
and flail through the air right into my grave.

All of this buzzing is often tied to screens, and almost
all of those screens are created by computers of some
kind (laptops, smartphones). There is the television too,
but that's a whole different thing because watching a
funny show on Netflix doesn't seem quite as draining as
drowning in the muck of a cable news channel.

I find the more time I spend on screens, the more
agitated and discontent I become. I start comparing
myself to people's profiles on social media. I get pulled
into negative news and dramatic commentary on the
state of the planet. I'm bombarded by advertising that

tells me I need to buy this or buy that, or do this or do that, when really everything is just fine in my life as it is. And sometimes I get really tired of the buzz.

🜋 🜋 🜋

I know there's a book out there about breaking your smartphone addiction, but how about breaking your addiction to screens in general? How about stepping out of this virtual reality we've created through the media and computers and technology, and instead being present in the moment? Maybe watching the sprays of branches blowing in the breeze outside your window. Maybe noticing the clouds rolling in as a springtime storm approaches. Maybe relishing in the quiet that envelops the air late at night, punctuated by an occasional cricket. Maybe listening to a great song on the radio that you haven't heard in twenty years, and that carries you back to a long-forgotten high school dance.

The problem with screens is they affect everyone around us; it's not just a personal problem if you can't step away. There are accidents every day because of screens in the car. There are fights with friends and significant others because of screens at the dinner table. Children get frustrated because of their parents' screens during soccer practice. Employees get in trouble at work because of screens during important meetings.

Even my cats are bothered by my screen time. Sometimes when I'm in the middle of petting them, I'll become distracted by the ding of a notification or the sudden need to research some random bit of information on Wikipedia that flew through my brain. And when I look up, unaware sometimes of how much life I have lost in that space, my cats meet my gaze with angry looks and swishing tails. Sometimes they've walked away entirely. They've learned that when Mama picks up that rectangular thing with the lights, she's a goner and it's just no use trying to get her back.

How often do we lose important moments because we can't say no to a screen?

I wish the smartphone had never been invented and yet I find it immensely convenient to be able to research something without having to go to the computer on my desk, or to send a quick text message to a friend to say "hello" without having to have a drawn out conversation. So I'm always striving for better balance. I try to monitor myself with software that tells me how much screen time I've tallied, where that time was spent, and how often I've picked up the phone. However, I find the monitoring just makes me aware rather than inspiring me to do something different, because there's a payoff to what I'm doing. There is *always* a payoff to any continuing behavior that brings an undesirable result to a person's life.

Personally, screen time allows me to avoid my anxiety—that's *my* payoff. The times when my usage spikes are when I'm the most fearful or anxious about something in my life, and I simply don't know what to do with that energy. My strategy these days is to just recognize the behavior and work to consciously step away as much as possible. I'm able to do this more when I ask myself, sometimes out loud, what I'm missing out on by losing myself in a stream of digital information. My answers are these: I'm missing out on all the free time that's stolen by the screen. I'm missing out on good books that I'm not taking the time to discover. I'm missing out on precious time with my cats who won't live as long as I wish they would. I'm missing out on new hobbies that might make me a happier person. I'm missing out on nature, which always centers and calms me. And I'm missing out on pursuing my life's purpose, because I'm wasting the time I've been given to get it done.

🍂 🍂 🍂

Put down the screen, people. It might be uncomfortable, but every change is uncomfortable at first. Let's get back to a world I remember from long ago—one where we picked up the phone to have conversations, where we sat down to dinner, where we allowed ourselves to think while waiting in line or at the stoplight. The best moments in life live in these spaces, you know. People, pets, the cycles of life, creativity, big ideas.

You won't find them in a screen.

MORNINGS ARE
IMPORTANT

*E*ven if you aren't a morning person, sometimes you should get up before the sun. I say this as someone who suffers from relentless insomnia and who spent the first thirty-five years of her life being a night owl. Getting up "early" for me was any time before 9:30 a.m., and going to bed "early" was 10:00 p.m. or maybe 10:30 in some years. But they say that as you get older, your body naturally starts changing its rhythm. You start getting tired earlier and waking up earlier, and sleeping less soundly. And you begin shifting from the habits of your youth into the habits of those who are many years into their journeys. Remember when you were a kid and you wondered why grandma was always up at five in the morning?

My theory about all of this is that your body is forcing you to look at what your spirit already knows: mornings are magical and nighttime is for peons. You need to get up and experience this part of life, because *this* part is where the good stuff is.

🍃 🍃 🍃

I woke up at about 5:20 a.m. today and couldn't sleep, which is not unusual for me but, even so, is always frustrating. I was so awake that I decided, since I saw a faint beam of light peeking from above my curtains, to just get up and catch the full sunrise this time. I often get up early when I can't sleep but I don't often get up before the sun (unless it's a dark winter morning, and even then I regularly find an excuse to stay in bed—"I'm tired" being the primary one).

I got up around 5:40 a.m. and trudged out of bed. I moved quietly to the bathroom and did my usual stuff—brushed my teeth, changed my clothes, pet my Maine Coon cat, Jack. He always comes to say hello in the mornings by rubbing against my leg, jumping up on the sink, and spreading his big body out on the counter while I brush my teeth. I scratch his head every so often and give him lots of kisses. I clean his left eye, which was already injured when I rescued him, and which goops up on him overnight. He purrs. He's a sweet spirit, this cat.

Sometimes when I get up extra early like today, he's confused, because just like humans, animals have routines and they pick up on yours. He can't see very well either, so sometimes he lurches his back a bit if I come prancing out and he's not expecting me. But today he just walked along with me as I quietly moved about my home, trying not to wake my husband who, incidentally, loves to sleep in.

I went and opened the blinds in the living room, wondering if I'd missed the start of the sunrise again. But today was different. There was a burning red in the sky far, far away as a new day peeked over the horizon. I stared a long time, picking up on the almost imperceptible changes of shadows and colors as I stood witness to the planet turning beneath my feet. I could still see one or two of the brightest stars up above, centered in the sky, and the moon shone like a lamp over to my right. I stepped out onto my tiny balcony and was greeted by a chorus of morning songbirds and evening crickets—the birds just waking up, the crickets singing themselves to sleep.

It was like I was in between worlds.

Between night and day, between waking and sleep. In that moment when different categories of time overlap and collide and blend into one another. I mostly noticed how quiet it was while the humans were still asleep, and thought to myself, *This is what being close to the earth feels like. This is what it must have been like long before I existed.* There were no cars rumbling, no airplanes flying, no people talking, no construction equipment growling. Just the birds and the bugs, and a red in the distance that grew slowly into orange, and then transformed into yellow and white.

If you never get up before the sun, you should because you're missing an extra special part of the day. I hesitate to call it "holy" because I'm more spiritual than religious these days, but it sort of is. It's on par with any memorable religious experience I've had, anyway. I sat there taking deep breaths, listening closely, focusing on everything around me, and I felt sort of like I was sitting by the ocean (which is my favorite place). I love listening to the waves crash, peering into the great expanse, looking with wonder at the earth and its power. This was just like that.

Unfortunately, the world is so busy (unless you live in the country and farm for a living) that you just … miss it. If you don't get up before the chaos, you miss your chance to find the steady current that underlies all of life. The tranquility that existed before we did, before any of us did, when the world was ruled by amoebas and bugs and reptiles and whatever else came before humans started stomping around.

I've decided that mornings are a way to reconnect with that part of life you start to lose track of as soon as you become an adolescent. As soon as your thinking brain starts overriding your dreaming brain, and the feelings of wonder and joy begin to fade and transform into pain and struggle and worries about the future.

As I've gotten older, I've tried to catch as many mornings as I can.

Now as an insomniac, I miss more of them than I wish I did. When you regularly can't fall asleep and then proceed to wake up all night long, getting up before the sun is not really on your to do list. *Sleep* is. And the same is true for people who are exhausted because of kids and jobs and caretaking and whatever else is occupying their days … and their thoughts … and their lives. It's hard to want to get up if your natural tendency is to hit snooze and bury your face in the pillow.

But it's also hard to go to church every Sunday. It's hard to clean your bathroom every week or two. It's hard to do laundry. It's hard to pay bills. But you do it anyway, and that's my point. You do it because you have to, or because you should. And why do those things get a "have to" or a "should" but taking a few moments to watch the sunrise doesn't?

🌿 🌿 🌿

I hope that as I go through the remainder of my life, I am able to find more ways to enjoy the mornings. To get up before the sun—not with the sun, but before it. To experience that peace and tranquility that honestly shapes my mood for the entire day. Even if I'm exhausted from lack of sleep, somehow that exhaustion is offset by those birds and crickets, those dimming stars and burning reds. Somehow I forget my stress and my troubles, at least for a while. And to me that's worth waking up for.

FEELING USEFUL

*E*verybody needs to feel useful. I truly believe that swirling around in all the talk about what makes life meaningful, you have love and you have relationships and then you have feeling useful. And this can translate to a lot of things. It can translate to the dependent relationships in your life, such as the way a mother feels like she exists for her child, or it can translate to other things in life like your career.

I spent many years working in corporate jobs as a technical writer, sitting in a drab cubicle without enough work to keep me busy for anywhere from 25 to 100 percent of my time there. I'd tap away at my keys, documenting random computer software that I didn't care about or trying to find a diversion on the internet—anything to distract my eyes from the clock on my computer screen. Time becomes really sluggish when you have nothing to fill it with.

When I was twenty-five years old, I actually went nine months at a job without a single thing to do—and most people at work knew it. I'd decided my boss kept me on the payroll mostly to preserve her image, but the impact to me was that I woke up every morning with a big stretch of nothingness in front of me. I brushed my teeth, made my oatmeal, put on my business clothes, and got in my car to trek across town to a job that was employing me for no reason. A job where I'd long ago exhausted every possible interesting article on the internet, every possible online game, every possible news site. This was before Facebook and smartphones, so I didn't have those to fill the time either.

I was completely isolated emotionally in that job too, listening to my boss cough on the other side of the cubicle wall, her lungs black (I'm sure) from the chain smoking. She maybe said "hello" to me once a month and probably only because she felt like she had to. Sometimes I would hang my head in my hands in despair, other times I would go out into the parking lot and wedge myself between two cars and cry, feeling like my life was void of purpose, like I was wasting my days, like I was wasting my life. But also feeling trapped because I needed the paycheck and I didn't yet have enough experience to find anything better.

I felt utterly and completely useless.

Eventually, I got tired of this scenario (the one of doing nothing or of doing things that didn't even matter) and became an independent consultant, hoping for something different but often experiencing more of the same. In one case, I was brought on at a corporation and then, after two weeks, was not given any more work to fill the time. I pressed tirelessly and was finally offered approximately three hours of work per week to do, and ultimately they decided they'd screwed up and let me go. After that I spent a couple of months working on a beautiful, carefully designed presentation for another corporation that was eventually tossed in the trash due to a change in direction. Talk about a punch to the gut.

These types of experiences burn into you after a while if you're looking for meaning and want to actually do something with your time as a human. In my opinion, doing nothing is pretty much the same thing as doing something that means nothing in the end (like the tossed-out presentation). I think it can be a form of slow torture.

So this is why I say we *all* need to feel useful. And I know this is true because despite the wonderful husband, the food in my pantry, the pretty decent roof over my head, and a couple of rescue kitties who bring me happiness, my life still feels off kilter when I don't feel useful at work, when I don't feel like I'm actually using my days for something that is meaningful to me, and when I don't feel like I'm using my talents in the world.

I've also learned that what gives people a feeling of "usefulness" is pretty varied. My husband does not see his job as a source of meaning, for example. He sees everything outside of it as meaningful and so he gets his usefulness there. And then I have a friend who is absolutely content raising her large brood of children and she has no need for a career in order to feel useful every day. She's all set at home with her kiddos.

The other personal issue I've had is a persistent need to feel like what I do during my days must be as meaningful as what I do when I'm off the clock. I've followed this belief to the point of trying to find some form of "greatness" in my career (you know, like being the next Oprah Winfrey or Ernest Hemingway) so that I would feel like my life was useful enough. And the problem with thinking this way is you don't see what you actually have in your life that's good, because it registers as mediocre in comparison to the vision in your head. So in the throes of my striving to be Oprah or Hemingway, I was missing the bit of usefulness right in front of me since it was taking a different form than what I thought should pass as such.

What I mean is that I'd become a small business owner after being independent for a while, and I found that, while I was rather unfulfilled on the whole because of the projects I was being offered, I was actually feeling somewhat useful by providing jobs to a couple of other writers like me. I strove to treat these people right, to treat them the way I wished corporations had treated me, and at the end of the day, I found a bit of meaning in that usefulness. Now this doesn't mean I found the secret to feeling useful in less-than-ideal work situations (like my nine-month stint with nothing to do) or that my business lasted (it didn't, although I gave it a super good run). In fact, I started writing this book because I still wasn't quite feeling like I'd met my "usefulness" potential. And I think that's what we need to pay attention to. Do we feel like we're not quite useful enough? Do we have a hunch that we're supposed to be doing something more?

These are your clues that you need to keep striving, to keep climbing. Personally, these clues are what drove me to dream about what could be possible for myself. To experiment. To put myself out there. To find ways to feel more useful by experimenting with what I thought might get me to a more meaningful place.

Because I think restlessness and discontentment are signs of a mismatch between your life and your true purpose. I heard this sentiment on a podcast once while I was long-term unemployed (again) and wandering amongst the trees near my home, wondering what the hell I was supposed to do. It really lodged itself in a corner of my brain and can be summed up like this: when you finally feel useful and you're content with how you spend your days, then you're using your life in the way you were meant to use it. If you haven't found that level of usefulness just yet, don't be afraid to keep striving for it.

I'm still striving as I write, and as I look for work when jobs fall apart, and as I try to be a good wife and a good kitty mom. And I hope that by the time I get to my last day, I can look back and feel like I found what I was looking for. That I felt useful enough to merit my entrance into this world in the first place.

I hope we all can.

IT'S OKAY TO NOT HAVE KIDS

When I was a little girl, I lugged a baby doll with me around the house and also whenever we were going somewhere to stay awhile—like when my mother had her counseling appointments and I had to sit in a dark waiting room, listening to Kenny G. In those situations, I also brought along a diaper bag with two fake bottles, some actual newborn diapers, and a change or two of baby clothes. I used to rock the baby back and forth, give it its bottle, pretend it was crying, and then subsequently pretend it fell asleep. This was probably around age five and about the time I had just started to come into consciousness as a human; I knew I existed as someone with her own thoughts and feelings (beyond just eating, pooping, and sleeping), but I didn't yet understand what was going on in my home life (the yelling, the crying, the bitter divorce, and the regularity of pinto beans or potato soup).

I remember wishing many times that I could take care of a real baby instead. I wanted to feed it, to cuddle it, to rock it to sleep—just as I'd done with the baby doll. And when that didn't happen, I asked my dad (on one of my weekend visits with him) to buy me one of those weird Baby Alive dolls that actually consumed "food" and pooped it out the other end. This made me happy until I abandoned baby dolls entirely a year or two later, when the idea suddenly no longer appealed to me. I'd decided I'd rather play with "grown" dolls like Gem and Barbie, probably because they were more like me.

I tell this story because it's the only time in my life I recall ever wanting to be a mother, and once that desire left, it never really came back. I sometimes credit this development to my experience growing up in a dysfunctional household. It was just my mother and me from the fifth grade onward, with me vacillating between feeling like a punching bag and feeling like a parent to *her*. My younger brother had gone to live with my father by that time, and I might have gone too, but my mother had (incorrectly) convinced me I wouldn't find any love there, so I stayed behind in the chaos.

Maybe something got turned off inside of me around the time I abandoned the dolls, and maybe it continued to be smothered as I grew up. I remember focusing hard on making good grades and going to college rather than on marrying and having a family. When I dreamed of the future and what my life might someday be, I of course hoped it would be one of happiness and financial security, but nowhere in that dream did I see myself pregnant and squeezing a tiny human out of my lower orifice. Nowhere in that dream did I envision afternoons in the kitchen, teaching my daughter how to cook, or evenings at baseball practice, showing my son how to catch a ball. Nowhere in that dream did I see anything, really, but me.

I'm not even sure I saw a husband because I don't think I believed anyone would ever love me enough. I did wish for something like a husband, though. My daily prayer before bed for most of my adolescence and young adulthood was, "Dear God, please let me have a good life and a good boyfriend. Amen." I was lonely and miserable. I wanted love and I wanted happiness. I didn't want anything else and I didn't think anything else would be part of that equation—not children, not anything.

☙ ☙ ☙

When I was twenty-three years old I became a sudden mother to a five-year-old. Even though I'd known my first husband had a son, I'd never really thought about parenthood until we were in court proceedings to secure custody. We'd honestly never talked at length about having children, but that morning a judge said we were awarded custody, and that afternoon we drove to the child's mother's house in the poverty-stricken side of town to pick him up for good. And that evening? I had a crying child splayed across my chest while his father went to work at the women's shoe store—kind of like Al Bundy but without the sarcasm.

When my stepson came to live with us, it was the first time since the Baby Alive days that I'd even had *thoughts* of being a mother. I was actually surprised by my excitement. I remember shopping for clothes and giggling at the miniature everything—the pants, the shirts, the socks, the shoes. I remember taking pride as I washed his new clothes, folded his jeans neatly, and hung up his shirts in the small closet at the corner of his bedroom. I remember smiling as we bought him good furniture and extra toys, and all the things he'd never had before. The process of bringing him home and caring for him awakened an instinct in me I hadn't previously thought I possessed. I would have jumped in front of a bus to save him without even taking time to think about it, and I'd never felt that way about anybody.

I took care of this little human for three years before divorcing my first husband for infidelity (he made me file the papers, even though *he'd* left *me*). And for those three years, I was a mother in every sense of the word. I felt it in my heart and it manifested in my life. I was "Mom" and he even called me that, and I liked it too. But after the split and the goodbyes, when I realized I couldn't be his mother anymore because I had no legal rights to be, it was like that side of myself became locked in a black steel box that burrowed itself deep into my gut. The trauma that was losing my son felt like it had irreparably broken me.

I used to tell people it was like my son had died but I was constantly seeing his ghost, because I'd still hear about him—or hear *from* him in moments of desperation when he was scared of his father (who was still dealing with some PTSD from the Iraq war). I loved him so much that I'd get sucked in for a moment, or for an hour, but then I'd quickly revert back to what was familiar to me: I didn't really want kids. Not anymore, anyway, if I ever did for a brief moment in time.

☙ ☙ ☙

As I began to rebuild my life and contemplate finding a new partner, I started to think my feelings about motherhood might be a problem for a potential mate. I mean, most of the world has kids. And this alone is why childless women can feel like such enigmas, and like something must be broken on the inside. Luckily it worked out that the man I met also didn't want kids. His reasons were different than mine (sort of), and so we rode off into the sunset together and created a fulfilling life that was quiet and peaceful, and that contained a couple of cats who are my kids with fur.

I've always liked animals better than humans, anyway.

Despite all of these positive developments, I went through a period in my early thirties where I became even more aware of myself as a non-mother, mostly as friends began to marry off and create little versions of themselves. I also had it thrust in my face constantly as a new bride, as friends and family berated us with, "So when are you two going to have kids?" (I wonder if my face looked like the Mona Lisa.)

At first I didn't want to own it. I didn't want to be that woman who said, "I honestly just don't want them," and get a response of, "*What?* How is that? You'll change your mind." (I've been told this before.) But after a while—and by a while I mean over several years and after transitioning into geriatric motherhood age (i.e., over age thirty-five)—I began to become more comfortable with the idea of going through life without leaving a little person behind. And I started to notice there were women around me (not many, but there were some) who didn't want to be mothers, either. They wanted to travel, or teach yoga, or pursue careers, or have a life built around themselves and their significant others. They didn't want the responsibility or expense or exhaustion of having children. And suddenly I began to think small thoughts, just here and there, that maybe it was okay to not have kids.

☙ ☙ ☙

I still have days where I struggle to accept myself for who I am: a woman who becomes annoyed by screaming children when I'm eating my Saturday lunch. I also still have days where I feel like I'm missing a chromosome, or like my childhood broke something in me that was originally there back in the days when I changed fake poop diapers for my Baby Alive. But even if that's the case, the end result is I'm exactly where I'm supposed to be. The end result is my life went in a direction that would have made it extremely difficult for me to be a mother. Tending to my health issues is a full-time job, and I would never have been able to write or to run my own business with children. I can barely do it with just me and my geriatric cat.

And when I'm brutally honest with myself, I'm quite happy with the way things are; I don't feel like I'm missing much. I like cats. Cats are quieter, they're less expensive, and they don't talk back when they're teenagers. I can leave them when I go on vacation and not have to worry about the extra cost or extra energy of trying to entertain them. In fact, I sometimes think about the last family vacation I took before my divorce.

I was trying to entertain a seven-year-old who wanted to go go go while also having no time alone with my partner. It was probably the most exhausting "vacation" I have ever taken.

One of my best girlfriends and I sometimes talk about not having children. She doesn't want them either, and she is relieved to have finished her duties as stepmom to her husband's now grown daughter. We both acknowledge that sometimes we feel like something is wrong with us, like we've missed something the rest of the world understands and we don't, or that we'll look back when we're old and feel like our lives were incomplete. But then we quickly change course, reminding ourselves that having kids is not a prerequisite for a fulfilling life.

And also, our cats are pretty darn awesome.

FINDING MEANING IN STRANGE PLACES

Some people find meaning in a church. Me? I've found meaning making memes for Instagram. Now stay with me for a second.

I spend a good portion of my life trying to figure out where meaning actually lies and how I can find it for myself. I've had meaningful situations or meaningful events, like volunteering on a Saturday morning or, you know, getting married. All of these things are meaningful to me, but they're also meaningful because it's sort of a given that they will be, or that they should be.

But what if you're an odd duck and you find something that suddenly gives you meaning but seems trite or silly? Do you go with it full force or do you turn away in embarrassment?

When I told my husband I'd started a hobby of making memes for my new Instagram account, he chuckled at me and said, "Memes? Okay." And rightly so. I get it. It sounds really silly when you take it at face value, just like that quirky ham radio hobby you have sounds a bit nonsensical on the surface. But it wasn't really about the memes themselves for me; it was about what I was trying to *do* with the memes. Or, more accurately, what the memes were doing for me. Because this silly little hobby channeled a part of my spirit that wasn't able to come out very often anymore due to work and obligations and ... life.

Every day I would plop down and cross my legs on my living room sofa, and I'd open up a free app I'd downloaded just for this purpose. It let me swap out pictures and change up fonts and typeface. There were different styles, different moods, different things I could lay over the top. It made everything into a miniature design project where I got to play with words and colors and shapes until the perfect mixture solidified and I had just the creation to express whatever it was I was feeling on the inside that day. And then I could hit "Save" and share it with the world in about five minutes. It was a quirky little bit of instant gratification.

I used my memes to share inspirational quotes or truths about life, or even short blurbs of poetry. I used the comments to tell a story about that meme or how it resonated with my personal life. I got a bit of a high when the little hearts showed up at the bottom of my Instagram feed, saying people "liked" my memes. Psychiatrists say this type of feedback is like a drug hit, and maybe it is? I've never done drugs so I couldn't tell you. But I would probably agree that those "likes" messed with my dopamine levels because I kept coming back for more.

Making memes gave me something to fully immerse myself in; it was something that made me smile while

I did it. Crafting those small creations also made me feel like I was a kid again, when I used to draw on construction paper or try to make origami animals, or decoupage a cardboard box in the quiet of my bedroom. In fact, I think I actually grinned sometimes during the process. And when I muse a bit on the time in my life when I was making those memes, I was in the midst of some real trials and tribulations. Creating them was a warm distraction that was probably good for my soul.

My meme hobby lasted for maybe two months before I dropped it and moved on to something else, but it wasn't meaningless even though it was temporary. It was useful for me because it served as a source of happiness in a bleak time, and it was apparently useful for other people because there were a lot of them who "liked" my memes. So my hobby had a purpose—as does whatever random hobby you engage in. That purpose may be for your own life journey or for someone else who stumbles across what you're doing.

Getting older means learning to look for these types of quiet occurrences—ones that don't always bring obvious tangible (or financial) results. Happenings you didn't see, people you didn't notice, points of view you never understood. And this includes looking for hidden meaning in random activities like feeding your cat or washing your car. Because life is just a series of activities, one after the other, and most of them have meaning (although that meaning is not always profound). Maybe it's just to distract you for that moment in time. Maybe it's to help you heal. Maybe it's to connect you with another human being you're supposed to meet.

So if you really enjoy scouring Craigslist for abandoned furniture, do it. If you really love looking at pictures of puppies while you drink your coffee, keep looking at those pictures. There is meaning there, because there is *joy.* And any time there is joy, you have found something worth following, no matter how silly it seems.

OWN YOUR
INTRO/EXTROVERSION

think there are two kinds of people in this world—the people who like people, and the people who hate people. Maybe that's a little harsh? The technical explanation (or so I've read) is that there are people who get energized by people and people who get drained by them. And then there are those occasional enigmas who flow in between: the people who seem to be equally at home by themselves and with others, equally energized or drained regardless of who or what is going on around them. But I've only met like one of those people. So I think that, in general, you'll fall into one category or the other.

I used to feel like there was something wrong with me because I was shy, or that something was inherently broken inside that caused me to be this way. I think you can be an introvert without being shy, but I really am a *shy* introvert. When I was growing up, I preferred spending my time with a roomful of animals (cats, dogs, hamsters, guinea pigs, birds, dwarf frogs) over subjecting myself to the humiliation of trying to make friends. In fact, I spent a lot of time shut up in my room, trying to create a refuge for myself when I really had none in my life due to my fractured family of origin. But it was also an early expression of my introversion. I felt better when I was by myself—even if I was sometimes lonely.

As I've become an adult and moved through my twenties and thirties, I've realized introversion is a part of my personality that has been there for a long time. It's not just that I'm kind of shy and a little embarrassed around other humans, but I also get tired when I have to do it a lot. I dread it. I find excuses, at times, to avoid it. This is probably why my teaching and training jobs made me feel like a drained battery, or why I've always been miserable in any job that required me to be in an office. I simply can't be surrounded by people (and meetings, and conference calls, and gossip) all of the time.

But I've grown as a person in that I no longer think it's a character flaw or that I have to try to change myself into something I'm not. I know it seems like the "accepted" and "cool" thing is to be an active extrovert. There is societal pressure to have 1,000 (5,000?) friends on Facebook, to get hundreds of "likes" on a post, and to appear to be popular even though you may not actually know a large percentage of those people. I also know extroverts are much less of a mystery because they have a more outward connection to society. They are the well-liked ones at the dinner table, they are the "life of the party," they are the people who you always want to make sure to invite back.

But the ultimate truth of life is that it's okay to not be like everyone else. It's okay to not have the job, the car, the lifestyle, the friendship list, the eating habits, the *whatever* of those you see around you or on television. And if you're an extrovert, great! There's nothing wrong with that; it's who you are and there's nothing wrong with you. So own it. But if you aren't an extrovert, own it too. Own it equally hard. There's no reason you have to be like the random acquaintance on Facebook who is always surrounded by fifteen people at large get-togethers. You simply don't have to be that way to be a valid human being.

Look around and you will see the world is full of people—introverts and extroverts—who all fill different roles and contribute in different ways. Just today I visited an awesome gluten-free/dairy-free/soy-free/refined sugar-free bakery. It was my first visit since I'd lost my ability to eat those things, and I was almost in tears because there was a place I could go where I didn't have to worry. A place where I belonged. I felt enormous gratitude to the person (probably an introvert) who decided she wanted to go experiment in the kitchen until she had enough recipes to open a place that could provide happiness to someone like me.

These types of moments remind me that who I am is just fine. That who I am is someone who is here to do something with my life. Our personalities are the surfaces of ourselves; our personalities are not really our souls … although they sort of are. They help determine how our souls move along across the earth, how they engage with other souls, and how they express our gifts.

The extroverts of the world may go on to become Oprahs or Lettermans, or maybe wedding planners or hoteliers. The introverts of the world may go on to become songwriters or researchers, or policy analysts or computer programmers. I'm sort of making these job titles up, because really you can do whatever you want. But the point is, you're made the way you are because it's the way you're *supposed* to be in order to accomplish the purpose of your life. So why fight it?

These days I don't force myself to engage in social activities if I don't want to, and I try hard not to worry about what people think if I don't. Because some people will understand you and some people won't. And some people in this world will like you and some people won't, no matter what you do. I mean, there are people who hate Shakespeare. And Hemingway. And Oprah (what?!).

So be proud of who you are, and go hide in your apartment with Netflix and a bag of popcorn to recharge if that's what moves your soul today. Then get out there and keep contributing to the world in whatever way that is, even if it's from behind a computer screen.

DO LOTS OF THINGS

*I*n my first corporate job out of college, when I was just twenty-three years old, the vice president of our department gave me some casual but poignant advice. He said to me, "When you're starting out, try to do as many things as you can. Don't do just one thing. That's how you get boxed into something before you know what you really want to be doing."

I remember sitting there in his office, turning his words over in my brain and thinking, *Okay, that sounds good in theory. But how do I make that a reality? I'm a project administrator with no experience in anything. I was one week away from total bankruptcy when I landed this temp job, and you want me to somehow convince people to let me try things? Right now I'm just trying to hold my life together without losing my dignity.*

But I took that advice and filed it away somewhere as I went back to my little cubicle. I pulled it out a few weeks later when my boss said to me, randomly, "I think you'd be a really good project manager, would you like to try it?"

She was one of the only good bosses I've had in my corporate career, because she saw my strengths and allowed me to experiment with them. This is what good managers are supposed to do (my experience is they usually try to step on you to propel their own careers—or maybe that's just what women bosses do, because women can be bitches). Even though I was convinced I would blow everything up, that I wouldn't be able to do anything I was asked to do, and despite the fact that the thought of running a meeting turned my blood icy, I said, "Yes." And ...

It didn't go well. Let's just get that out of the way. I crashed and burned and politely excused myself from future project management opportunities.

It wasn't that I couldn't do it successfully with a bit more grooming, I honestly just really hated being a babysitter to men in their forties and fifties. Who was going to listen to a shy twenty-three-year-old when they were behind on deadlines and didn't give a rat's ass because, truly, many of them seemed to be overworked or hated their jobs anyway?

Still, being open to the new job experience and trying it allowed me to flow around between a few different things while I was there. And so by the time I left, I'd written manuals, designed training classes, and turned down a permanent job as a trainer (the day before signing paperwork) because my soul just told me it wasn't right. I remained a temp worker and pissed a few people off, but I still have no regrets about that.

Go with your gut.

I moved from there into a career as a documentation specialist, which is a fancy way to say "technical writer." And the truth is I still got stuck; I was a technical writer for six miserable years and couldn't seem to will or beg my way out. As I've already mentioned in this book, some companies didn't have enough work to keep me busy since I plowed through things so quickly. Other companies hired me to fix some documents and then actually didn't need me anymore after that. So I sat around staring at walls, wondering where the meaning was in my life, and not understanding how I was in this predicament when I wanted to work hard and do something good.

I did hang on to that VP's idea of not doing just one thing because, as often as I got the courage to do so, I kept asking for new things to try. I failed and succeeded to varying degrees, bouncing from job to job, trying to find something that would challenge me and feel right, something that might show me the direction I was actually supposed to go in my career considering, honestly, I still had no idea.

Even when I finally accomplished the "thing" I'd thought I wanted to do for many years—working for an ad agency—I still wasn't satisfied. I got tired! I felt myself longing for the days of my "leisurely" technical writing endeavors as I sprinted through agency work, which was relentless and exhausting. This nostalgia for a job I once despised was even more confusing to me. I'd achieved my goal, but I wanted to go back to the boring career I'd had when I hated my life? Something still wasn't quite right.

I often feel like people who watched me go through this flailing around must have labeled me as flaky. I would try this, try that. Get tired of this, get tired of that. For a while, I had totally random aspirations. I was going to be a jewelry maker for a period of about eight months, and I invested in hundreds of dollars' worth of beads and wire and tools. I set up a business name and a website. I bought packing and shipping supplies. I spent hours practicing and posting pictures of my creations, saying I was now going to be "Sterling Gemstones" (my business name) and this would be my new life goal. I sold two or three pieces and then ... meh. I got bored.

I don't want to do this anymore, I thought. *I can't stay hunched over this mat, chasing beads that keep flying off my table, trying to twist a wire into a perfect arc. This is maddening. It's time for something else.*

Then there was photography. I even went so far as to get paid for professional commercial photography by one of my writing clients. I was first sent to east Texas (only a couple hours' drive from my home in Dallas). Then to Austin. Then to San Antonio and Houston. Then to Tulsa and Oklahoma City. And finally, all the way to the farmlands of Wisconsin. I did this work over the span of about a year and thought maybe I'd be a commercial photographer in my second life. But the energy slowly drained out of me and my enthusiasm sailed away on a river. I found myself dreading the work—even *avoiding* the work—mostly because I was sure my pictures would be an embarrassing portrayal of what I was not, actually, able to do. I enjoyed it more than many other things I'd tried, but I still hadn't found my match.

I've also been a yoga teacher (I struggled to find work), a schoolteacher (burned out in less than a year), and a corporate trainer (yes, eventually I circled back to that same type of job I'd rejected at age twenty-three, and—wow—was I as miserable as I thought I'd be). I've tried writing fiction (two failures), and young adult novels (one failure), and a memoir (in progress, maybe I'll finish editing it). I've thought about being a baker, a chef, a psychologist, a social worker, a nutritionist. Then for a short period I was going to be a life coach. You get the idea.

I've tried some of these things to varying degrees by reading about them or even enrolling in grad school (I dropped out after two classes, of course). As of today, my longest "try" is with running my own small writing business, which lasted nine years before I had to give up and go back to corporate life. And I don't even pretend to think my current job will be what I do forever, because I seriously don't know.

And to be honest, I wouldn't change anything about this weird journey of mine. Every career turn prepared me for every successive job, almost like I was being guided down a scripted path. I did my project management to learn how to run marketing campaigns and a writing team, I did technical writing to sharpen my brain and learn how to write succinctly, I use my knowledge of psychology to figure out how to position my copy ... and so on and so forth.

Everything I've done so far (well, except the jewelry making) I've been able to bring to the table in some fashion and use toward my life today. So even though

I got stuck sometimes and appeared flaky to everyone around me, I'm not sorry I lived my life that way. And I'm not sorry that I'll probably live the rest of my life that way either.

As we make decisions, most of us try to consider what we will and will not regret by taking each available path. Still, sometimes the only way to figure out if you like something is to do it. On the other hand, sometimes the only way to figure out if you *hate* something is to do it. Then for people like me, who lack innate confidence, the only way to figure out who you really are and what you're capable of is to sample different things and see what sticks. I call it "throwing spaghetti on the wall."

In order to try different things, you have to abandon the thoughts you have about what you *should* be doing with your life and just be okay with whatever it is you are actually doing. Sometimes this is the hardest part of all, especially if society (or your family) is telling you what you are "supposed" to be doing and making and buying. This doesn't mean you should accept mediocrity or live a reality that doesn't suit you, but it does mean it's okay to do things other people may not agree with. It's okay to quit that job you hate and try something else, even if you just started that job two months ago. It's okay to set up a company name or buy a random website domain, and then change your mind later.

It's also okay to completely change careers, to abandon that expensive law degree you got when you were twenty-six in favor of the culinary pursuits you really want to follow when you're forty-five. We can't truly know ourselves when we're that young (at least most of us can't), so why do we expect to know the entirety of our careers? Or our lives? We haven't even begun to get started when we're that age.

And this is probably why that fifty-something VP advised me the way he did, looking at a naïve girl sitting in his fishbowl of an office. Perhaps he wished he'd done things differently and wasn't stuck where he was sitting. Or perhaps he *had* tried many things and was happy with where he landed. I'll never know, but I suspect the former.

I do remember I encountered him a short while later in an elevator, surrounded by his colleagues, and he asked me how things were going. "How do you like it here?" he'd asked. I told him it was nice that people didn't have sticks up their butts. I realized immediately this was not the right thing to say (why would *anyone* say something like that?!), bowed my head in embarrassment, and avoided him for the remainder of my short tenure at the company. I'd been so miserable in the job that I had nothing positive to conjure up, and so "sticks up butts" came out instead.

And this just tells me how much I needed his advice at that time in my life. I still didn't know enough to mind my verbal garbage before spewing it out in an elevator full of executives. I had no idea about the challenges that were ahead, both personally and professionally, and how easy it was to get stuck in something you didn't want to be doing. But he knew.

I went on to have many terrible jobs that would leave me crying some days and feeling like a slumped-over, banged-up bag of dirt. I used to run outside and sit under a tree and cry. Or hide in my car and wipe tears away. Or go to the bathroom and sniffle in a back stall. This went on all the way into my thirties until I finally got the courage to use that huge bag of skills I'd accumulated and go off on my own. And even then, I failed and I cried.

I wonder, now, would I have been so open to different things if that VP hadn't advised it? I can't be sure, but I do know we should take in as many new experiences as we can while we're here. Don't spend your energy on buying things, spend it on doing things. Don't stay in jobs you hate, keep it moving. You may hate the next job too, but that's okay, move again. The experiences you have are what shape your life, your happiness, and your overall feelings of contentment as you move from one day to the next. Your career is not excluded from this process and, in fact, is a huge part of it.

So who cares if you come off as flaky? I don't call it flaky. I call it intuitive. I call it not settling for crap. I call it experimentation in life. I call it good.

STUFF WILL STILL
BOTHER YOU

*O*ne would think, by a certain point in life, that the things people say or do would just roll off your back. But the truth is: they don't. And even the most seasoned and positive person will still have things that bother them. These could be things related to friends, family, partners, work situations, children. Any time a person strikes out at you or treats you with meanness, it's going to hurt or make you angry because that's simply the human condition. The goal, then, is to learn to move through those feelings more quickly so they don't stick around and muddle your entire day, week, month, or life.

🍃 🍃 🍃

I've been interacting with someone for a few years who has, over the past few months, started to drive me crazy. And I'm not just being dramatic or creating hyperbole; everything went downhill after a petty argument followed by some sort of hurt feelings and a refusal to respect my decision to engage in the relationship differently going forward. I should insert the following note: we are all allowed to have boundaries. Some people get pissy when you try to set them, however.

The relationship has now broken down to the point where I feel constant hostility, where I'm ignored, where I'm greeted with a short temper—when I'm considered important enough to speak to, that is. I've reached a point where it's started to negatively impact my self-worth and dignity. And this is quite disappointing in some ways because I've worked for decades to stop caring about what people say or do.

When it comes to this sort of scenario, I've tried all the standard strategies to talk myself out of not letting the things other people do bother me. I've done the cognitive behavioral therapy route, where I forcefully tell myself (in my own brain) that what a person says or does is not important. That it does not define me. That it should not have the power to change my mood. And I say this to myself over and over again; sometimes it works and sometimes it doesn't.

I've gone the meditation route, where I sit quietly and watch my feelings ping-pong around in my brain. I feel the anger, the stress, and the anxiety rise up from the depths of my soul and spill into the pit of my stomach, and then I tense up with dread at the memory of what happened or at the upcoming interaction I have to have with this person. As I watch it all, I try to rise above. I try to tell myself these feelings are there but they are temporary, and I can choose to disassociate with them if I want to. But even if I'm successful in the moment, I'm often a disaster when I have to re-engage with the person later.

I've tried journaling, which my long-time counselor has advised me to do when I'm upset about something or someone. This sometimes includes writing the person a letter, spewing all my feelings from the depths of my psyche, and then ceremoniously folding said letter and sticking it in a drawer on my nightstand. If you've never tried this before it can be a really powerful therapy and I highly recommend it. But for the really hard stuff, the stuff that hits me deep, the letter-writing practice sort of turns the temperature down on my feelings rather than turning off the burner entirely.

I've also tried talking to my husband and friends about those times when people hurt or anger me. Hearing words outside of my own head helps to calm the unease inside of me. It reassures me that I'm okay, and that the words and actions of other people don't matter. It helps me to let it all go and move on to other things. And again, depending on the situation, this can either be effective or it drifts out of the other ear.

The honest-to-God truth is that sometimes *none* of this stuff works—especially when I'm dealing with memories of abandonment or am experiencing injustice. And in the situation with the person I described previously, none of it has worked yet. However, I do continue to try my strategies when those old hurts well up or when someone pours cold water on my heart. And I think we all can get to a place where we become less upset and less off balance as we work on fortifying our inner strength.

A prime example is my husband, who is really good at this. In fact he's good at a lot of the things I struggle with, but we come from different backgrounds and have had different life experiences. His approach to the world is built with a different set of rules. In the nine years we've been together (so far), I've rarely seen him thrown off by the actions of others. Things people say or do just roll to the side and don't even touch his inner sense of self. This is his normal. However, he is not impenetrable.

There was a time when he resigned from his job of thirteen years—one where he had worked his ass off and was the epitome of dedication, never with any kind of complaint about his work or his personality—and he was greeted with vitriol by his boss. This shocked and also deeply bothered him. He became angry (he's rarely angry) and fell a bit off center. For a couple of days, at that, which tells me none of us are infallible. But his experience also tells me that we can all keep working to try to be more impenetrable.

❦ ❦ ❦

I've been reading a lot about Buddhist practices lately, and the teachings explain that our feelings and reactions are a part of the human condition we can learn to transcend. It just takes continuous trial and error, and a commitment to separating ourselves and our emotions from those who throw sticks. Because honestly, sometimes people just like to throw sticks. It could be because they're mad at something else and you're an easy target, or it could be because they harbor their own self-doubt and hurling things at you makes them feel better. Maybe it makes their discomfort and pain a little easier to deal with. It could also be that they recently got sticks thrown at *them*, and the only thing they know how to do is throw sticks at you in order to divert the negative energy elsewhere.

Most of us know these life truths about how humans can behave when they're in difficult situations, but sometimes we forget them when we're overcome with anger, sadness, or embarrassment over what someone else did to us. Learning to look at reactions more objectively—and to separate ourselves from them—is definitely an ongoing practice. And isn't all of life simply a practice anyway? If we'd figured everything out right away or early on in our journey, what more would there be to learn? What purpose would there be in existing at all?

These are greater existential questions, of course, but I think one thing we can do while we move through life is to cut ourselves some slack. If your boss pisses you off even though you've been working hard to "let go" of whatever comes, don't become disappointed in yourself when you get mad and stay mad for a little while. Maybe get frustrated with yourself if you use the opportunity to lash out in retaliation, but don't be disappointed in your feelings.

I use my own emotional responses as a teaching tool to work on my journey. They allow me to gain awareness into my internal processing and to improve my personal monologue. They also serve as a barometer to help me understand what is really going on, and whether or not

I need to remove myself from an unhealthy situation. If I simply can't get past what someone is doing, and if it's simply unacceptable to me or it hits me so deeply in my gut that something tears inside, then I know it's a sign I need to cut ties.

Humans are capable of spewing toxicity in incredible ways, sometimes tainting everyone and everything around them. Sometimes you just have to walk away from that sort of thing, because no amount of positive thinking can tilt the balance in your direction. And this is okay too.

Going back to my aforementioned toxic relationship, where this person is now impacting my sleep and my health, I now know I need to make an exit. And in this case I'll be able to do so. However I'm also a realist, and I know walking away isn't always an immediate option for everyone. Most of us are stuck in certain situations (especially when dealing with money and survival) until we can find a way out of them. And that's okay. But in the meantime, make a plan. Give yourself a deadline to walk away. Break up with that friend you've known for twenty years. Start looking for a new job. Join Meetup.com to find new friends. Volunteer at a nursing home to fill the void created by your abusive mother. Or maybe offer yourself something nice—perhaps a piece of chocolate—every time you are treated like shit by the person you have to continue to engage with in the short term.

Doing these sorts of things helps me feel like I have the upper hand *on the inside*. Like I am working to take back control of my feelings and my world, even if it's done slowly and step-by-step. I think this alone can help us take some power back and claim our own positivity, our own emotional health. There is strength in making a plan, and nobody can take this away from us; it lies within ourselves.

I've already gotten a plan together to cut ties with this person even if doing so leaves me isolated for a bit. Should I be able to tolerate what's going on without these sorts of temporary bandages? Maybe. But *my* truth is that in this situation I can't, so I'm going to do what I can do—make a plan, put it into action, and eventually get the hell out of dodge.

Sometimes life is just too short to deal with bullshit.

THERE IS NEVER A PERFECT TIME

I've spent a good part of my adult life waiting for the perfect time to do the things I want to do. I think this idea of "the perfect time" is pretty common for most humans. Some people wait for the perfect time to have a child. Some people wait for the perfect time to leave a soul-sucking job. Some people wait for the perfect time to pick up and move to their dream house near the beach. And some people wait for the perfect time to mend fences and rebuild relationships.

I'm ashamed to say that I've spent many years now (we're closing in on a decade) actively avoiding the things I want to do. I do it partly because of ongoing struggles with depression and anxiety, where I spend my off hours pacing around or engaging in meaningless distractions to avoid my neurotic mind, and I do it partly because I'm afraid to fail. *If I fail,* I wonder, *then what can I dream about?* Dreaming about the future sucks up a lot of my energy and also provides a sense of hope to cling to. I hold on to a belief that maybe once

I achieve my dream, something magical will happen in my life. To attempt now and fail would leave me lost and unsure of myself.

I also avoid things because I'm afraid to succeed. At first I thought "fear of success" was such a silly notion. Who is afraid to succeed? But honestly, with success comes change, and pressure, and expectations, and uncertainty. Some of these feelings we put upon ourselves, but some of them are feelings thrust upon us by others. For example, I tell myself quite often that if I achieve my dream (writing a book) and people like what I do, I'll have to produce another good book. After all, my publisher will want me to, I will want to, and it's my dream to do so. But what if my second book is not as good as the first one or as well-loved? What if my initial success—and the feelings (doubts?) it stirs within me—cause me to absolutely fall flat on my face? Or what if my second book is just as successful, and I have to try again to "one up" myself as I go along on my journey as a writer? Can I really keep that up? And what if I can't?

Fear of success.

And then I circle back to, "it's just not the right time." I had that exact thought this morning when I felt like I wanted to write but told myself I didn't have the mojo. It's a Tuesday, and on Tuesdays (and every weekday) I have to focus on my day job since I am not a trust fund baby or married to a millionaire. But as I sat on my patio in the breeze (I work from home), eating my mid-morning snack on a rare August day where it was cool enough to be outside, I decided the conditions I was looking for in order to work on my book are sort of already here today. And they exist despite what I was continuing to say to myself, which was: *I'll be able to write when I don't have to worry about money. When I don't have to work a day job that sucks my energy away. When I have quiet around me and no interruptions while I work. When the weather is soothing—maybe cloudy or rainy. When I feel calm in my mind rather than like I'm in a perpetual game of Pong. When I'm not in this city and I'm instead looking at some nature.*

Well, living somewhere else aside, today the only thing preventing me from doing the thing I want to do is *me*. Today I don't have to worry about money. I'm actually on retainer right now and waiting on my client to get back to me, so it's kind of like having a job but not having to do anything (at least for the moment). Today my husband went into the office, which he does per company rules just once or twice a week, so I do have the peace and quiet I need. Today it is also cloudy and overcast, which tricks my mind into thinking fall has arrived. And the change in weather always brings me a renewed sense of calm and peace as I transition into cuddling up on my sofa under a fleece blanket, with a candle flickering in the fading daylight. Today I also feel rather calm instead of anxious or jittery, probably because I did a walking meditation before I sat down to work this morning.

Excuses. Fear. Procrastination. Waiting.

The truth is, I've written quite a bit when the conditions weren't right or weren't even *close* to being right, including a poem that was selected for publication in a literary anthology. It was just that on those particular days, I got out of my own way.

❧ ❧ ❧

Getting in your own way is part of the complexity of being human. But if you can't get out of your own way regularly enough, sometimes you simply run out of time. Sometimes infertility strikes and you've exhausted your options to have biological children due to age. Sometimes the economy crashes and you're stuck in that soul-sucking job until the next recovery. Sometimes the housing market surges and you've been priced out of a dream house on the beach.

And sometimes people die before we get a chance to tell them we're sorry.

There is simply never a perfect time in life to do things. If you don't just go ahead and do them, you'll wake up one day as an eighty-year-old woman, wondering what the hell happened. Wondering why you didn't pick up running when your legs worked, or why you didn't change jobs while you still had the chance to rebuild a new career, or why you didn't have kids when you were young and energetic rather than when you were older and better off financially.

If you're waiting for the right conditions to present themselves to do something you want to do, perhaps you're waiting for conditions you don't actually *need*. Or perhaps most of those conditions are already there and you simply aren't looking at them. Personally, I don't intend to keep waiting for things to be "right" because honestly, there is no right. There is no perfect. Life is constantly changing and fluxing and we all just have to float on a raft in the middle of it all, focused on the things we want to do, while the water moves around us and we rock side to side.

So do those things you set out to do. Examine why you hold yourself back and whether or not those magical conditions you seek will ever actually arrive (maybe they will, maybe they won't, maybe it doesn't matter anyway). Don't wake up in the winter of your life and kick your own ass for waiting too long. Even if things slow to a stop for a while and you aren't moving in the direction you want to go—which will happen from time to time—it's probably temporary. Whatever you're meant to do will keep calling you until you do it. Don't be so stubborn that you block yourself from becoming a fully-expressed version of yourself. Go and do that thing you came to earth to accomplish.

Me? I'll be over here, writing.

FRIENDS FOREVER?

*I*t took me until I was in my late thirties to understand that friendships change over time. Even the best of friendships. You know, the ones you think will always be just the way they are right at this moment. Close, fulfilling, easy, natural. And perhaps I thought this way about friendships because I grew up without very many lasting ones, so I didn't learn those lessons until later on.

❧ ❧ ❧

When I was a young girl, the overarching theme of my childhood was loneliness. I have mental snapshots of myself playing alone in my room with my dolls, or sitting by myself on the floor with my cat or guinea pig or rabbit, or walking outside in solitude to look at the trees on a summer afternoon. I didn't know how to make friends back then and I didn't know how to be one either. Maybe some of this self-imposed isolation was a product of my home environment, or maybe it was borne from my introverted tendencies. It's hard to know. Even as an adult, I still wonder how much of my introversion is simply a product of my early formative years. "Nature versus nurture," they say.

I didn't make my first real friend until fourth grade. Her name was Ella and she lived on the wealthier side of town, with houses that had light switches shaped like flat Vs instead of protruding arms. She was Chinese and an immigrant, but I didn't see any of that. I saw a friend. Because of her I, proudly, learned how to count to ten in Chinese and also how to repeat her mother's *nǐ hǎo ma* when I would call. Ella used to tell me that one day she would take me back to her country and show me everything she remembered. We'd go together, forever friends, arm in arm and all grown up.

Our friendship lasted until the fifth grade.

My second friend came in middle school, perhaps the most painful time in my adolescent life because I was made fun of constantly—everything from my haircut to my clothing to my lack of breasts. It was especially brutal in choir, where the girls took aim at my singing to the point where I just mouthed the words instead. Meeting my second friend, who we'll call Paige, was one of those situations where the two most scorned kids in the school came together to form a secret alliance. I was poor with a bad home life, crooked teeth, and questionable hygiene. Paige had good hygiene but was overweight, had a bedridden mother, and lived with a very strange beanpole of a father.

This friendship is the best memory I have of my childhood up until high school. It illuminated what were some very dark days for me and probably kept me from finding other less healthy means of escape. With Paige, I finally got to experience some of what the other kids my age had already been a part of for years. I found someone to talk to on the phone for hours. I got to attend a sleepover, even though it was just the two of us. I got to stay up all night giggling about boys and eating Funyuns and drinking Mountain Dew. I had someone to talk to about body image and the myriad of issues that come up in that stage of life.

She was my very best friend.

For a year or two.

I was young and when you're young, fitting in is more important than secret alliances you've vowed to keep. As the more popular kids began to back off their ridicule of me and pile it onto her instead, I joined into their chorus with the hopes I might finally be accepted. This resulted in me losing my friend *and* still being the scorn of the school, because the pendulum swung back again when they'd used up that punching bag and needed another. I remember apologizing sincerely in high school and we did reconnect somewhat, but things were never really the same. And we never spoke to one another again after my disappointment in her lax Maid of Honor duties when I was twenty. I can't say I blame her after all that had happened.

My other friends in high school gave me a taste of real friendship (meaning, the kind that lasts longer than a year or so). I remember gravitating toward Asian students, apparently for the second time in my life if I think back to Ella in fourth grade. I can't think of any logical reason why I did so because I attended a very diverse school and minorities were never ostracized. But I felt completely at home in that group despite our obvious physical differences. (I was a mixed-race kid who sometimes looked white and sometimes looked Hispanic—people still ask me about it to this day.) Nobody looked at me any differently and I didn't think of myself as different, either. It was nice to feel like the outsider who had finally found a place to belong.

I still have contact with some of those high school friends today, but only superficially and through social media. I had hoped maybe those relationships would last forever too, but they all moved on and made new friends. They fell into what seemed to be idyllic college experiences that followed the guidelines of how college was supposed to be—fun, carefree, friendship-driven, and memorable. For me, though, college was a disappointing blur that consisted of splotches of transient acquaintances, several part-time jobs, a lot of reading (being a lit major is very time-consuming), and a too-early marriage. I moved around a lot too, attending three schools by the time I graduated and not really feeling like I fit in anywhere.

The only real friendship I formed in the four-and-a-half years I spent in college was during my first year, with a slightly older male student who lived on the boys' side of the dorm. He harbored a love of music (piano and violin) shrouded in a more practical computer science major, and we spent hours in the evenings chatting on AOL—or "America Online" as it was still known at the time—back when instant messaging was a brand-new thing. This friendship was on-again-off-again beyond my college days, but eventually fizzled out when he professed his undying love for me after I got divorced eight years later. I unfortunately did not return the sentiment.

I think it's accurate to say I didn't form my first true adult friendships until well into adulthood. I was in my late twenties and newly single, flailing around and not knowing where to land, and I'd made a conscious decision that I'd better become a little more outgoing to avoid fading into obscurity (you know, just disappearing like I had never existed at all, because nobody even knew who I was).

So I made some friends from work. How, I honestly don't recall. I must have been propelled by a nuclear level of distress to reach out to those people on a personal level. But it was these friends who took me through some of my worst, lowest years. It was these friends who became my confidants, who shared in my adult problems (and my adult beverages), while otherwise walking through life on our tiny little slice of the planet. Some of my favorite memories from my late twenties are actually of our hours-long talks about life and purpose while sipping wine over dinner.

I thought these people would be my close friends for the rest of my life because the relationships had far surpassed anything I'd experienced in high school. It all felt so real and so permanent; we all seemed to think about life the same way and we all had the same goals. In fact, as the years rolled by, I realized these friendships had snuck past the decade mark.

This, in my mind, was as good as forever.

But as of this writing, I no longer see any of those people on a regular basis. In fact, one of them I haven't spoken to in years. Two others moved away, and as a result the relationships fell into a slow decline. Another long-term friend abandoned me when I got remarried in favor of other friendships with single women. My situation had changed, and she decided she was out.

I was in my late thirties when the last (and best) of those important friendships finally fizzled due to distance, and it was then that I finally understood the whole "friends forever" thing is a fallacy. At least, the idea of remaining the same *kind* of friends forever is a fallacy.

🍃 🍃 🍃

Friendships seem to go in and out like the tide, usually based on life circumstances. Sometimes they change when kids arrive. Sometimes they change when one person moves across the country. Sometimes they change when someone gets married, or divorced, or is faced with a serious illness. Sometimes they change when one of the friends grows (or stumbles) internally, and decides they are no longer interested in a friendship with the other person.

Losing those first adult friends was a humbling and heartbreaking reckoning for me. I felt naïve and stupid for not understanding that almost nothing in life is permanent—friendships included. I didn't realize that a commitment from a person in one moment does not equal a commitment for a lifetime. Missing this rather obvious life truth made me feel very foolish, like I was in elementary school again, alone and not understanding why.

I suppose it's rather cynical to view all friendships as possibly transient, despite how strong they might be in the moment. But perhaps it's only cynical if you want to label it as cynical. The other way to describe this approach would be realistic, and that's the way I'm choosing to look at it now.

As much as it hurts when something we love ends or someone abandons us for reasons we don't understand, it seems to be the nature of life. Two people in any relationship (romantic or platonic) are like two trees growing side by side. Do they both grow up together, at the same pace, reaching for the same place in the sky? Or does one tree grow sideways, diverting and following another path that suddenly seems more interesting? Perhaps, sometimes, one tree dies midway through the process or is hacked down by a random axe.

Nothing is certain or predictable in any relationship, and I finally began to feel better when I saw these developments in my friendships not as a poor reflection on myself and my ability (or inability) to be a friend, but just as a natural consequence of being human. Sad events and disappointments are a part of life, and a faded friendship is just another one of those. And when a friend finally exits our lives, do we choose to sway in the breeze, keeping an eye out for the next kindred spirit who will sprout up beside us for the next part of our journey? Or do we fold over and crawl back into the soil, hiding our heads in despair and blame?

I'm learning, slowly, to sway.

YOU DON'T HAVE
TO DO HIIT

I spent most of the first twenty-two years of my life as a dancer. Not a pole dancer (I would hope not at age three) but a ballerina, a jazz dancer, and a tap dancer. I was very active in general and even played softball up until high school, and when I stopped doing that, I was lunging with fitness celebrity Denise Austin in my living room and later taking jazz classes in college. I'd always bought into the idea that you had to hyperventilate and break a sweat or it didn't count as exercise.

After a hiatus in my early twenties, I became a hip-hop dancer and then a salsa dancer, which kept me in shape and is also how I met my wonderful husband. But part of what happened when I became chronically ill during my thirties was I was forced to let go of the need to focus almost solely on calorie burn. I'd always believed any activity that didn't burn more than one hundred calories—like taking a walk or doing some easy yoga—didn't count as a form of exercise and was simply a waste of time.

HIIT (high-intensity interval training) and boot camps are all the rage right now. So are 5K runs, spinning classes, and other forms of bodily torture that promise extreme calorie burn (five hundred-plus an hour) and do, in fact, keep us healthy if we pursue them in moderation. But the thing nobody talks about is the negative side, like the people who are so addicted to the burn that they can't let their bodies rest. The people who use exercise like alcohol to soothe something broken inside. The people who won't stop running obsessively, even though their doctors have warned them of knee replacements or torn ligaments. They just *can't* stop.

I've never been one of these people, but I would say I viewed exercise in the wrong way as a young adult.

⊘ ⊘ ⊘

My grandmother used to walk at least three miles a day and that was the extent of her activity most of the time. She would complete several laps around the local mall because she was elderly and because sometimes it's an inferno in Texas. On occasion, she would attend an easy water aerobics class at the local college—mostly because she liked how she felt (weightless, light) in the swimming pool. She wasn't worried about calories. She was worried about mobility and about doing something she enjoyed that would extend her mobility as long as possible.

I never remember my grandmother concerning herself with how long she exercised in the time I knew her. She just focused on consistency and showing up, working hard to keep moving with her arthritis, and ensuring she could continue to live independently as a widow. And at age seventy-five she was still mobile, still had all of her mental faculties (I attribute this to her voracious appetite for books), and was still in pretty good physical shape considering her age. What got her in the end was her anxiety (she fretted so badly that it spiked her blood pressure), a guy who almost ran her over in a parking lot (and left her with injuries she never fully recovered from), and a very aggressive cancer (which spread through her brain and eventually took her life). Physical fitness was not her demise.

It took me a while to learn from what she modeled to me. In fact, it took me a while to come back around to exercising at all after I started spending five days a week in a corporate office and then had mommy duty in my early twenties. I was just too overwhelmed and tired, and was overcome by my own inertia. This is the only period of my life that I recall not being active in some form—except for the occasional twenty-minute yoga DVD—and what I remember most about that time is that I felt *terrible*. I was sluggish and bloated. I had a bit of a stomach and no muscle tone anywhere. I overate every day, despite hating how I felt afterward, and I struggled to go to sleep because my digestion was overwhelmed by junk. I was ashamed of what I'd become after having been so strong for so much of my life.

After my divorce, I was free to reevaluate and start anew. I got in touch with my body again and noticed how young I still was (twenty-six). I considered how I ought to feel physically but how weak I actually was.

I also realized I was missing a part of myself by not dancing anymore; dancing had formed so much of my identity until I got sucked into the vortex that is adulthood. So I faced my anxiety about large groups and enrolled in some adult classes at a local dance/yoga/ Pilates studio to give it a go.

🍂 🍂 🍂

At first, I had a healthy approach to my return to exercise, because I was only trying to get my strength and endurance back. But as might be expected of a newly single twenty-something, within just a few months I began obsessing about my figure, about how often I was doing cardio (versus something else like yoga), and about whether or not I had done the cardio long enough to look attractive. For the next few years, I sometimes pushed myself beyond my limits. I stomped ferociously on my mini stair stepper that I kept in my living room, I attended hour-and-a-half-long dance classes several days a week, and I danced the nights away on the weekends. I was skinny, for sure, but I was also obsessed and trying to assuage my own insecurities through constant movement. In my mind, I needed to keep my figure through any means I could. This required me to tally my cardio sessions on an internal scorecard and to make sure I met quotas every day and every week. I continued this practice even after I started dating the man who would become my second husband, because I had lost a husband once before and I would do anything to keep this one from leaving. If I maintained a thin enough figure, I reasoned, maybe this one would stay.

And this, my friends, is where I—like so many of us—began to go wrong. Exercise should not just be a means to a calorie-burning end or a way to make someone love us more. It should be something we enjoy and that feels good to our bodies.

After I got sick at age thirty-four, I was humbled to find that my body was no longer within my full control (had it ever been, really?). In fact, I couldn't make it do a lot of the things my mind wanted it to do, including dancing and stair stepping and sprinting. I no longer had the physical energy for those activities even if my mind was demanding I meet my quotas.

By age thirty-five, my stomach was a patchwork of surgical cuts. My abdominal muscles felt stuck together, and I couldn't even bend in the same way as before. I still wanted to have that beautiful figure I'd once had, but my body was having the final say. It was tired and demanded I stay still.

The next few years are what changed my relationship with exercise and what also helped me to understand that I didn't have to do HIIT or forty-five minutes on the stair stepper for my workout to be "valid." I learned to find contentment with, and to give myself credit for, just being able to walk. I eventually came to allow walking to be my primary form of exercise, and one that I elevated in validity to the maniacal exercise sessions of years past. I also allowed yoga—any kind of yoga, not just hardcore (and calorie-burning) Vinyasa flow or Ashtanga—to be my secondary form of exercise. Because in truth, I couldn't even get through one of those hardcore classes anymore. I'd tried to go for about two years and spent many of them sitting back on my heels in child's pose, resting, for what felt like at least a third of the time. Eventually I couldn't even do that anymore and was lucky to get through fifteen minutes on my mat at home. It was a real blow to my ego.

As I watched myself now hobble through life instead of run, and as I let go of the need to count calories and tally my time, I learned that it doesn't really matter so much *what* exercise you do. What matters is that you do it, you consider it valid, and you find it enjoyable—no matter what it is you choose. What good is running if you feel like throwing up every time you run? Is this really what your body wants you to be doing? Perhaps you should take up tennis instead so you can sprint in little bursts. Maybe your body would be happier that way.

My body is currently happy with me walking on the days I can physically manage it and adding in yoga when I have enough energy reserves. I rarely break a sweat anymore because it usually makes me sick when I do, so I don't concern myself with doing it at all. I just remind myself that I'm still showing up, that I'm still trying, and that maybe next week I'll be a little stronger and can do more.

The lesson in all of this is: you don't have to be a spin cyclist, or a marathon runner, or an HIIT boot camper. You *don't*. You can just be a walker, like my grandmother and me. Or a yogi, like many friends I know. Or you can do whatever other activity speaks to you—gardening, bicycling, roller skating—it all counts. It's all exercise. There is no prescription for "correct" or "good enough."

IT'S SOULMATES (PLURAL)

I've heard that the concept of soulmates can be traced as far back as Plato's *Symposium*, dated circa 385 BCE, where the poet Aristophanes says Zeus cut people into two pieces and now each new person wanders the earth looking for their other half. I think a lot of people still believe in one soulmate because of how the concept has been described throughout history. But looking at it in Plato's way, if you then miss your person or if things don't work out with the one you've chosen, you've hit a *Press Your Luck*-style whammy. It's over, you've lost the opportunity to experience a divine connection. Things will never be the way they're supposed to be and you'll slowly drift off into a dark tunnel of loneliness, never to return. If this is your approach to life, it's perfectly okay. I used to have this approach as well. But these days, I don't think there is only one soulmate given to us in life.

Let me explain.

❧ ❧ ❧

When I was growing up, my idea of a soulmate had just two qualifications: it would be male, and I would marry it. The end. I didn't believe a soulmate could come in any other form and I didn't believe I could accidentally marry anyone but my soulmate. I think it's easy to subscribe to this concept when you're young and haven't experienced the loss of someone special. And I'll also say there are people who marry their soulmates at eighteen and go on to celebrate fifty- or seventy-five-year wedding anniversaries. This is real too. But as I've gotten older (and gotten divorced), I've decided I don't really like the concept of a single soulmate as my personal truth.

The first problem is that if we can only have one soulmate—because, sorry, that's all we're allotted—then every divorced person has either screwed things up with their soulmate or has messed up and married someone who wasn't their soulmate at all. Neither of these explanations is satisfactory to me; I simply refuse to believe that most thinking people could marry someone with whom they don't have a meaningful connection beyond a romp in the bedroom.

The second problem is that if things go wrong in a relationship, it means you've either wasted your one soulmate opportunity or you still haven't found it at all. What if a person is sixty years old and gets divorced? Has that person lived for sixty years on this earth without a soulmate? Or worse, with a *fake* soulmate?

Beyond the male-female (or male-male or female-female) bonds we establish in our romantic relationships,

I've also come to understand in my own life that a soulmate can be platonic or some other version of a loving connection. In fact, I can say with some amount of confidence that I've had at least three soulmates during my life, and possibly a few more. There's my husband, of course, but there's also my beloved cat Mimi, and my grandmother Norma.

How did I come to this conclusion? I define a soulmate based on an energetic connection that is not found in other relationships I engage in. So, for example, I believe my husband is my soulmate not just because I love him dearly and chose to marry him, but because one day I went down the hall to chat with a neighbor and my husband couldn't find me. And during this time, I felt pangs in my chest and stomach, and an overwhelming feeling that he didn't know where I was (I'd told him where I was going, but apparently he'd nodded off). I kept brushing off the feeling as anxiety. When I finally did return home three hours later to a frantic man who had searched everywhere for me, I understood what it all meant: I felt those pangs because we have an energetic connection. I was picking up on his panic at exactly the time he started panicking, even though I had no information about it.

I've seen this sort of thing happen with other husbands and wives, especially in dire medical situations where one person can pick up on the feelings of another. But I also experienced it myself with my grandmother on her deathbed, when she suddenly awakened at the sound of my voice. She looked at me with those beautiful blue eyes and tried to tell me she loved me (or something else), but couldn't get the words out. There was a collective gasp in the room and I remember a cousin saying, "Did you see that? Did you see what she did? She opened her eyes for you!" It lasted for about fifteen seconds and she slipped back into unconsciousness. It would be the last time she ever woke up.

🍂 🍂 🍂

There are a few other stories I have just like this, about connections with select people or pets in my life. And as I've gotten older, I've realized those connections are divine connections—or energetic ones. They go beyond the fleeting relationships or acquaintances we make as we go through life and instead have distinct characteristics that seem to transcend time or distance and even death. These connections, I feel, are what define soulmates.

And the good news is that if you come around to the idea of there being more than one soulmate put on this earth for you, you can feel certain you will encounter more along the way. So if you just had a falling out with your best friend, then perhaps she wasn't supposed to stick. Or if your marriage failed, that doesn't mean you're doomed to never have an amazing connection with another human being ever again.

And anyway, not everyone has to be a soulmate to be a valid person in your life. Not every person you date or even marry will automatically be a soulmate and perhaps not every pet will be one either. But every interaction you have with another being is worthwhile. They all take you further down your path, they teach you something you need to know, and they show you how to be a better person in relation to others. I think most of us have so many wonderful connections to other humans that maybe trying to peg certain ones in a "soulmate" box is not a good use of our time.

Maybe we should just look at them all as blessings.

NOT EVERYONE
GROWS UP

I like to think most people reach a place of maturity where they finally let go of pettiness, unwarranted rage, silly behavior, and downright meanness. That eventually they grow out of whatever negative habits they have. That they learn to approach situations with maturity. That they think things through with reason, and then respond with kindness (or at least polite words). But the truth is, many people never do any of these things. And I think it's especially hard to come to terms with this immaturity, of sorts, when you suddenly see it in someone you used to love or admire. This often happens when you keep growing but that person stagnates and is left behind.

☙ ☙ ☙

I was on the freeway today minding my own business, listening to the radio and watching the concrete whiz by. I was in the left lane and driving just slightly above the speed limit (as I am apt to do) when, suddenly, a car raced up and then slowed down dramatically behind my bumper, weaving slightly like a drunkard and flashing its headlights. For a second, I thought maybe the driver was trying to flag me down because something was wrong with my car. But I realized quickly, as I saw her wide-open mouth flapping, that this wasn't the case at all. She was actually screaming obscenities (I assume) and flashing her lights at me in anger.

This went on for a good two to three minutes but I remained calm and undeterred, although I did shake my head at how silly it seemed to be. *Just go around me, it's pretty easy to do and there is nobody in the way.* But the next time I looked in my rearview mirror, I was horrified to find the flash of her cell phone flickering as she snapped pictures of my car. One time, two times, five times. More screaming, more hand gestures through the windshield. At this point, I felt something shift in my stomach because we all know when something feels wrong or dangerous.

I moved over to the middle lane to allow her to zoom past me and out of my life and, I'll admit, I debated whether to duck like a coward or risk getting shot in the head—because my brain goes there these days in America. But I didn't do that and instead peered timidly to my left as she approached. I was astonished to see her filming me, the flash of the camera steadily white, angrily narrating whatever she interpreted the situation to be. Then she hit the gas, swerved in front of my car as if to make a point, and sped off—in the middle lane at that. It was never about the left lane or about *me* being there.

Is it ever?

I was shaken enough to call the police and ask for the non-emergency operator so I could share my story and ask what to do. I'm not one to want my license plate searched for online so a gang member can come and blow me away as I take my evening walk. (Of course, I also like to catastrophize things. It's sort of a fatal flaw.) But I was absolutely unnerved and I didn't know what the fallout would be.

The whole situation sort of played into my current levels of paranoia and fear that I think many Americans share with me. I've been more on edge as I've watched a lot of bad things on the news over the last year, both locally and abroad. I've watched grown men behave like pigs, I've watched strangers spew hate, and I've seen reports of random violence or, honestly, random idiocy. As I sit now and reflect on all of these things and on my driving experience this afternoon, I can't help but come to the conclusion that some people will just never "see the light" about their behaviors, as we might say. Some people will remain immature and will let their emotions take over at their own peril. Some people will fail to see the consequences of their actions and how everything they do sets off a line of dominoes in all directions. In fact, some people will never grow into better versions of themselves at all.

I've learned to try to let go of people like that. I can't change them and I can't make them see what they refuse to look at, just like I couldn't make that silly woman in the car—a woman who most definitely was *not* an emotionally-driven teenager—see that what she was doing was an absolute waste of her time and energy. But what I *can* do is try to find compassion, even when I don't want to. I *can* ask myself why the negative and hateful people of the world act the way they do. And I can *also*, sometimes, feel sorry for those people instead of angry. Then I can move beyond all of that and try to empathize once the emotions wear off.

☙ ☙ ☙

It's been a few hours since that woman created my first starring role on camera, so my shaking has stopped and the anger has evaporated. Now I've come to feel sorry for her and to also wonder what in her life made her so unhappy that she attempted to spread her fear and misery to a stranger. I'm glad I'm not living in whatever torment she is living in (whether it's a bad day or a bad life). I now feel grateful instead.

I think it's the job of the more emotionally or spiritually mature people of the world to put as much good energy and positivity forth as possible. We can start by trying to understand rather than getting carried away with the negative energy created in us via an emotional response. And that's not to say we can always understand everything. I cannot understand someone who murders another person—and I don't think I should have to. But I *can* try to understand what situations in the world might cause people to do terrible things (poverty, fear, abuse, violence) and then make sure I work to improve those situations. I can also make sure that whatever energy I put out is as positive as it can be, because everything we do adds to (or takes away from) the state of humanity.

So I do hope that lady has a better day tomorrow. I hope she can find some peace in her life and come to terms with whatever darkness is eating away at her soul. Not because it's easy for me to say that about a person who rattled me so much, but because it's the right thing to put out into the world.

WE HAVE TO TRANSITION

Sometimes I think about the dancing days of my youth. I remember flying through the studio in a majestic *grand jeté*, or lacing on my tap shoes and performing my favorite time step, or rolling across the floor in a lyrical dance that my teacher had just choreographed. Then as a late twenty-something, I remember spinning on my toes at midnight at a salsa dancing social and laughing as my partners swung me around. I remember the hip-hop classes I took on Thursday evenings, where I moved my body in ways I'd never explored before and then drove home in the dark, covered in sweat.

Dancing is what made me the happiest for a good part of my life and it was something that defined me for a long time. "Oh yeah, Elizabeth is a dancer!" I liked being called a dancer. I took pride in it, like I was something special. And I still claimed myself as a dancer until about age thirty-one, when I stopped taking studio classes and wasn't keen on staying up late anymore to dance salsa.

Dancing, like many other things in life, is a physical activity and is therefore limited by age. Any active person will lose some of their power and stamina as they grow older, even if they can still tap their feet or shoot a basketball. I like to think of my dancing in the same way as anything else that people love and simply can't hold on to for their entire lives, whether it be sports, or a particular hobby, or studying at a university, or spending time with their grandmothers. Some things in life just don't last and they aren't meant to, and we all have to learn how to transition.

❧ ❧ ❧

I have a few distant acquaintances who, despite the passage of ten or fifteen years, seem to be living the same life in perpetuity. They're still going to the same places on Friday nights, still hanging out with the same people, still eating the same food, still working in the same jobs. In these particular cases, it's like their lives have stagnated to a place that may or may not be an ideal one (that's not for me to judge); it's simply the place they have settled into. And that's not to say hitting cruise control is inherently bad. I firmly believe that all beings on this planet—both human and animal—need a routine to depend on. Our entire Earth and solar system are built on the routines of seasons, revolutions, wind patterns, sunrises and sunsets, births and deaths. Most of us do not flourish without some sort of routine.

But I think sometimes we get stuck. Maybe we're afraid, maybe we're stubborn, maybe we lack the internal motivation to do anything but just coast along.

Or maybe we don't want to deal with change, because change is inherently uncomfortable and sometimes we simply can't face it, even if we know we need to. I know that used to be true for me.

⚘ ⚘ ⚘

I used to throw fits as a child if anything in my life had to change. I demanded my room look exactly the same as it always did, even as I grew out of my pink floral canopy bed and my white lacquered desk with its imposing bookshelf hovering over the writing space. Even as my growing body no longer fit within these pieces of furniture, and as my emotional development no longer matched the childish print of my bedspread, I still desperately clung to sameness because I think it gave me a sense of control in my out-of-control home life.

And I feel like when you do things like holding on to items or routines that no longer suit you, you can coast along for a while before the universe shocks you out of it for your own good. I believe if our hearts are open to whatever is best for us, and if we haven't stepped out of our carefully cultivated plot of land on our own, then the earth will begin to shift beneath our feet when it's the right time. *Move,* it will say. *It's time.*

For me, I coasted along until my life imploded in my twenties and the ruins of divorce set in. And from then on, I began to embrace change as often as it decided to come. That embrace has grown more loving and more secure as time has worn on.

This is not to say I don't have my moments. When my best friend moved out of state, I resisted that change (internally) for a while. I didn't want her to leave, and I didn't like that she wasn't here with me anymore. But for the most part I've grown comfortable with change so that when I think of my dancing days, for example, I no longer feel a longing or a sadness for them. I miss the way I used to feel physically and I miss the feats I used to be able to accomplish with the power of my legs, but I also embrace the things that are different about my life now. Different is not necessarily worse, remember. It's just … different.

❦ ❦ ❦

We all have to transition and let go; that is the nature of life. Our grandmothers will eventually die and we'll have to learn to live without them. Our knees will eventually hurt such that we can no longer run up and down the field and kick a soccer ball in a competitive game. Our brains may eventually fail us and it may be harder to do those Sudoku puzzles that we love to do. Our kids will eventually grow up and we'll have to learn how to redefine our lives without them.

And what we can do instead of being saddened by these ongoing changes, instead of feeling a loss, is to embrace what *is*. We can embrace that we are growing older, which affords us a great amount of wisdom that not everyone is privileged to receive. We can embrace that we are now spending time with our toddlers instead of with our girlfriends, because having a family is pretty great too. We can embrace that life constantly brings new opportunities and new challenges, even as those we used to know and love drift off (sometimes abruptly) into the sunset.

There are days when I miss being able to twirl on my toes in pointe shoes, or play softball, or eat the foods my stomach could still digest once upon a time. But most of the time, I don't even think about those things anymore. I have other interesting pursuits in my life now. I read really great books, I watch old movies on Turner Classic Movies that bring me happiness, I socialize with people who expand my horizons, and I am a mom to a couple of rescue kitties who fill my heart with warmth. I also have a wonderful husband who I get to share my days with, and travel with, and lean on in the hardest of times (like when that best friend moved away). And these are all good things that are different than the life I lived before my body got a bit older.

When we can view changes as different and as part of the natural course of things, it somehow makes them easier to handle. They become less like a loss, and more like just the way life is.

YOU CAN READ MORE
THAN ONE BOOK

There are a lot of people in the world who only read one book. And I mean this both literally and figuratively, depending on who you're talking about. Some people only see things from the point of view they were taught as children, or from the one they picked up through their circle of friends. They dogmatically believe their perspective is the truth, despite the occasional presentation of contrary evidence— although people who are in this frame of mind can't see that evidence anyway. People who only read one book walk a very narrow path with twenty-foot tall cement walls all along the sides. There isn't even a shoulder to pull off on.

I grew up Catholic because I was born into a Catholic family. Most of us are either automatically planted into our families' religions or are never introduced to religion for the same reason. When we're small we don't have a choice in what to believe. Religious or otherwise, we believe the things we are told to believe. If Mom says the garbage disposal will send a knife flying at our face (true story), we believe her and stay away from the switch. We don't have the capacity to reason for ourselves and decide that maybe what we're being told is a crock of crap. We go along with things until we become adolescents and teenagers, and maybe at that time we start to branch out. Or maybe we don't. It really depends on where you come from and how strong your parental influence is.

Some of us continue to live under the umbrella of our parents for much of our lives, and there is nothing inherently wrong with that—if it makes you happy and if it doesn't cause you to treat others in ways that are mean-spirited or hateful. Some people go through their entire lives never straying outside the boundaries of what they were taught as children. And this is okay. But it's also okay if you want to read a different book. If you want to see what else has been written by people outside of your sphere of influence, maybe of a different culture or of an entirely different belief system.

🍃 🍃 🍃

When I was about sixteen years old, I decided I wanted to learn about Christianity outside of Catholicism. It helped that my mother didn't make me go to mass regularly anymore, so the idea of exploring something new was less of a big deal than it might have been otherwise. Plus, I wasn't venturing way off the path that had been laid out before me at my birth. Protestantism was still a denomination of Christianity, so I began to attend a local Church of Christ where my childhood friend was a member. It was there that I also spent time with my boyfriend, who became my first husband, and where I got involved in a youth group for the first time. I learned Protestant Bible songs and went to Bible study. I had no idea that what Protestants sang in their church was completely different from the "Eagles Wings" and "Taste and See" songs of the Catholic church. I also didn't know that people sat around discussing the Bible outside of what was read by the priest at mass.

In my early twenties, in the throes of my marriage falling apart, I finally decided to be baptized as a Protestant. Back in my youth group days, there'd been some well-meaning teenagers who insisted I was going to hell because I was sprinkled rather than dunked. This had stuck with me through the years and, in some ways, I think I decided to be dunked in a tank as a sort of insurance policy. In other ways, I think I was looking for salvation from the pain in my life; my first husband had come back home to work on the marriage, but it was imploding anyway. I was feeling deeply inadequate. All of these things are more valid reasons for my approach to the dunking tank than was my belief in God. Although I did have a strong one at that time, for sure.

When my marriage fell all the way apart two months later and I found myself alone, without a husband, without my stepson, and not sure of what to do, my religious beliefs finally began to crumble. I'd read this one book my entire life—the Bible—and I'd done everything it said to do to achieve the promise of happiness and peace and an eventual seat in a beautiful new world filled with white light. Yet there I was, feeling exceptionally miserable, utterly alone, and staring at a life that really had been full of nothing but pain and sorrow. This was true despite not only my strong faith, but my determination to live according to Biblical teachings and my weekly attendance at church.

It wasn't in this moment of sudden aloneness that I lost faith in God, and I didn't lose faith forever, but He did slowly fall out of my favor as I struggled through my next few years. I had my first drink at age twenty-six and proceeded to drink every weekend after that. I had sex outside of marriage because, well, that's what the world did and I was not going to marry someone just to have sex. I *was* going to be in a relationship before having sex, though, and not sleep with random people. I did still have some morals.

I cussed, which I'd never done before. But even the "F" word wasn't strong enough to capture the emotions that were swirling inside my body. I listened to gritty rap music that was not at all wholesome—not at all like the Christian songs I'd previously swayed to while I drove home from work. And to tell you the truth, I didn't feel the least bit guilty about any of it. Maybe this is what we feel like when we rebel? I hadn't had any of that during my teenage or young adult years, so I suppose it hit me in my late twenties when I was truly alone for the first time.

I tried once or twice to go back to church, although I chose a nondenominational one this time around. What I'd observed earlier in my life were people who were supposed to believe in the same thing, but who were segregated by different versions of said thing (Catholic, Presbyterian, Methodist, Episcopalian, Baptist, etc.). So I decided I was going to go about it in a different way and find a place with no formal affiliation. This led me to a new experience entirely.

Not only was I no longer in a church with stained glass windows, candles, and statues of Mary alongside various saints, but I wasn't in a wooden pew at all. There wasn't a cross on the wall, or a cappella singing, or Bible study in an adjacent room. I was in a dark square building with flashing strobe lights, a live band, attendees in jeans and tees, and a pastor who gave his sermon via a very large movie screen (because he actually preached at a location twenty-five miles away).

At first it was refreshing to feel like I could go and just be spiritual without having to worry about my physical body and what I looked like. But at some point, the newness wore off and I realized that nobody really spoke to me. I didn't know the songs (or like most of them all that much), and I missed some of the sacredness in the air of the old churches I had previously attended. When my life didn't change for the better despite my dedication to church-going—when I continued to not be able to find work, to cry my heart out in loneliness, and to face financial catastrophes—I dropped out again and went home for good.

I didn't go back to any sort of church for a long, long time. And to this day, I still only go to church when I'm asked to by family members—usually on holidays. What I did instead was read other books. And I mean this literally and figuratively, of course. I started looking at other people's lives and how they lived them. I started giving validity to different points of view and different ways of living. I stopped looking down on people who said they didn't actually believe in anything and weren't sure what happened when we died. I stopped believing that being a Christian was part of an exclusive club that granted its members restricted access to the good things in life, because honestly it hadn't worked for me anyway.

And I know there are people reading this who will say, "But! But you don't really *know* God. You did it all wrong. You didn't have enough faith. You didn't wait long enough." And that's fine. We're all allowed to believe anything we want. But we also should not take it as a personal affront when someone believes something different, and if we do take it that way, I think it's a good wake-up call to examine ourselves for ways to be more tolerant while still holding firm in our beliefs.

As for me, I decided to stop caring what others thought and just explore. And that exploring led me all over the place. I decided that not only can we read more than one book, but we can take the things from each of the books we read and decide what makes sense to us. It's similar to how we can look at a friend, and at something he or she is doing in life, and decide it is good. We can also look at that same friend and decide another thing he or she is doing is bad or destructive. We can emulate the parts we like, and disregard the parts we don't. This applies to all of life and, I feel, to religion as well.

Religion is a great compass. It is here to help guide us to peace and happiness, and to help us make sense of the world while we are here. It offers us morality and tells us how to treat others. It keeps us focused on what is good and right, and on the ways we should be spending our time. But it is also a great divider and, I would venture to say, one of the greatest dividers on earth. And why is that? Because some people believe there is only one book.

❧ ❧ ❧

I like to read lots of religious texts now. I've read yogic texts, which existed long before any religion, and I've read Hindu texts. Lately I've read Buddhist texts and, of course, I still sometimes read the Bible. I've also read poetry by Rumi and Robert Frost, and literature by Ernest Hemingway and W. Somerset Maugham. All of these books provide me with perspectives on life that I can pick and choose from, and decide which makes the most sense to me personally.

Being open in this way has not only allowed me to become a more tolerant and accepting person, but it has also allowed me to find forgiveness and meaning where I couldn't find it before. It has helped me traverse the mountainous pathways of my life, find stillness in the anxious moments, and let go of old pain from the first few decades in which I existed. It has also helped me to find God in the version that jives with my own approach to life.

The "books" you read are everywhere. They are in the people you meet and in what you experience. They are in the literal books you study and in the conversations you undertake with your pastor or your grandfather.

We go through life constantly learning, with some of us more open to new knowledge than others. And I hope more of us will learn to let those concrete walls fall off the sides of our paths. We need to see each other's roads too, so we can better understand ourselves in relation to the entire human race—our friends, our loved ones, the strangers we cross paths with, our religious allies and foes, and our enemies too.

BOOBS WILL SAG

I've been fortune that, as a woman with no children and a B-cup bra size, my boobs didn't start to sag until my late thirties. And, really, this happened when I lost a bunch of weight due to chronic illness. I had blown up to a C while I was thirty pounds overweight, and then my lady parts magically deflated while the rest of my body dropped the toxicity it had been carrying for a few years. Because, of course, the boob fat gets sucked out first.

I used to do the pencil test. I read about it in a magazine once—it's where you take a pencil and hold it horizontally, and then you stick it under your bra-less boob. If it falls to the ground you're still good, you've still got sufficient perk. If it stays put, then it's doomsday for you. You've started on the downhill slope (literally) and it won't get any better from here.

Go ahead, you can pause and try it. I'll wait.

Some women have to deal with boob saggage and other signs of aging much earlier in their lives. Genetics play a role, pregnancy plays a role, stress plays a role, and lifestyle plays a role. In my late twenties, I went to a nightclub with two women who were kindergarten teachers. This alone was astonishing to me—apparently they partied four nights a week!—but the other astonishing thing was that they were both only around twenty-five. These girls looked like they were closer to forty because of their partying and no-sleep lifestyle, which had left its mark on their youthful faces and started turning their bodies to stone long before it was time.

☎ ☎ ☎

Getting older is never easy, I don't think, no matter your age. And it's not just the physical part. There are also the energy changes, the hormonal changes, the mental/memory changes (what did I eat for dinner last night? I seriously can't remember), and the sudden desire to burrow into your couch on a Friday night rather than head out to meet friends. As someone who is just at midlife, I can only speak for what I've experienced so far. But I do wonder if the early parts of aging are slightly harder to get through than the later parts.

Now stay with me for a moment.

I'm not saying a little boob saggage is harder to deal with than memory loss or osteoarthritis. But what I *am* saying is I think it can be especially hard to let go of the idea that you are young—that you are beautiful (or at least decent-looking enough), that you have most of your life ahead of you (and therefore you still have time to dream), and that you can abuse your body in order to do the things you feel like doing (i.e., staying up late, sharing a bottle of wine with your friend, attending a university while somehow working full-time, or committing yourself to two jobs so you can make ends meet). I found that my early- to mid-thirties were a major life transition that felt particularly challenging when it came to aging. And this was *before* I failed the pencil test.

ᘒ ᘒ ᘒ

We don't often think about how the superficial parts of life sustain us. How that random compliment on our appearance helps us get through our days or overcome the spiteful remark our ex made last week. Maybe it even helps undo the damage we've stored up from years of being made fun of in school. It certainly did that for me. I was the awkward girl with the crooked teeth, bushy eyebrows, and oily hair. I had bad clothes (because we were poor) and no friends (because I'd been pegged as a loser), and then, in my late twenties, I discovered that other people actually thought the opposite of me. Eventually I began to feel less awkward.

Identifying as "pretty" felt rather redeeming after spending so many years identifying as "ugly" and "unlovable." I liked posing for pictures with friends and then studying my carefully applied smoky eyes or my toned dancer's legs. I liked that I could go up to any man at the salsa social and ask if he wanted to dance, and not be turned away very often. It was a nice self-esteem boost that sustained me through some really hard times when everything else felt like it was falling apart. But the problem was that as soon as my body started aging, and as soon as my face started showing more of its years than it had before, I began to panic a little bit. I was happily coupled by that point, but I still felt a loss because I'd liked the attention I used to get. It had made me feel valuable as a person and like I was worth something, as shallow as that may sound.

I no longer wanted to take so many pictures in my thirties, and I no longer was proud of what I saw when I did. When I first lost weight from being ill, I stood in front of the mirror and cried. There I was, even smaller than I had been in my late twenties, and all I could do was despair over the two deflated balloons stuck to my chest that seemed to perfectly match my graying hair and sallow skin. My husband, of course, told me that was rubbish. Even though I'd already been on a multi-year journey of releasing control and accepting things (both physically and mentally), it took me a few more months to lose my sense of shame. I needed time to embrace the new me and to come around to being okay with the loss of some youthfulness in my face, the accelerated graying of my hair, and the brand-new sagging of my formerly-perky boobs.

🦋 🦋 🦋

I guess I look at my breasts as a sort of symbol that represents everything we go through as we age. I haven't gotten too far along in the process yet, although sometimes it feels accelerated (chronic illness has a way of doing that), but I feel like I have a good understanding of what's to come. And I'm glad I've been able to (mostly) make peace with the changes in my body. It's nice to find my value without a self-absorbed fire that needs to be stoked by external compliments and perfectly-posted pictures with a bunch of "likes" on Facebook. Instead, it's a value based on who I am, what I can do, how much love I have to give, and how many life struggles I have survived.

There are a few celebrities who I notice build their entire personas around their appearances. And what happens, I often wonder, when the beauty starts to fall away? When they can no longer fake being younger than they are? When their looks can no longer be revived by creams or exercise or medical procedures? Will they retain a sense of self or will they feel completely lost and no longer valuable as a human being?

Getting older is our fate, if we are lucky enough to do so. And as women, it can be really hard to watch ourselves change and transform. We are constantly subjected to what is deemed "beautiful" by the collective media consciousness and it sure isn't what we look like most of the time. But I think it's just a process we each go through—men too. Some people are able to come out the other side and age gracefully and with dignity, while others get dragged along, kicking and screaming, until the day they die.

I'd like to be in the former group, not the latter. There are too many wonderful things in the world to see and do, and after everything I've learned, I'm sure not going to waste my energy worrying about my aging skin and my graying hair. Or how I no longer look the way I used to look in pictures. Or how I'm starting on the downhill slope of life and catcalls are a long way off.

I'm also not going to worry about my sagging boobs.

THE INSECURE SELFIE

I used to be the Queen of the Selfie. In fact, my husband (before we were dating) used to comment on how often I took them. "You take the most selfies of anyone I'm connected to on Facebook," he said. At the time, I was kind of lost in that physical beauty thing I've talked about. I thought I looked pretty and I was capturing it so others could see it too.

All. The. Time.

But there was a deeper goal I was trying to accomplish and that I didn't really understand until later: I was trying to get attention, to get "likes," to get compliments. I wanted validation that I was in fact as nice-looking as I thought I was, or as I used to be, or as people commented to me sometimes. This was all a ruse to distract me from the nagging feelings of self-doubt and insecurity that were plaguing my internal consciousness. Deep down, I wasn't totally convinced I was pretty or worthy or part of the world. I needed the constant reassurance that this was the case. So I took selfies. Almost every day.

I see people now who do it in excess like I did, and I wonder what their motivation might be. I often think the behavior must be prompted by some sort of deep insecurity like it was for me—an insecurity that maybe they can't reach or that they don't know is there just yet. I think the bubbles of insecurity can be simmering just under the surface without you really being consciously aware of it, because it's really hard to face those sorts of feelings.

When I was in the throes of my everyday selfies, I remember feeling like I was pretty confident in myself. Perhaps, I thought, the most confident I'd ever been in my life. But then if that was the case, why did I have such a need to have my pictures validated by comments, "likes," and compliments? Was I really that confident at all?

🍃 🍃 🍃

Selfie culture is a really new thing. When I was in high school, we of course had cameras, but we used them in a totally different way. Pictures of ourselves were often done as part of a group or as a pair, or sometimes as a single shot that you'd asked your friend to take of you standing near something you wanted to remember. If you were going to waste one of your thirty-two pictures on a potential failure (i.e., an attempted picture of yourself, taken by you, later known as a "selfie") it was probably not a good use of your 35mm role. It was better to have someone else take the picture you wanted—and only one—because you had to ration what you had. And this meant you weren't so focused on how perfect it looked or how you looked in it. You just wanted to be in the picture.

❦ ❦ ❦

When I was around thirty-two, I was at a baseball game with a bunch of friends and sitting in the stands near third base. We were behind a couple of teenage girls and they were obviously less interested in the game than they were in their phones. I watched one of them, perhaps seventeen years old, try about fifteen times to snap the perfect selfie. When she finally got one that seemed good enough, she then proceeded to edit *everything* out of her face. She zoomed in on a pore, airbrushed it out, zoomed in on another, airbrushed that one out too. She did this all over her face, creating tiny targets out of every minor imperfection she found and destroying them with the touch of a button. But that wasn't enough, I guess, because after her pores were finished she started tweaking her eye color. Then the shape of her face, then the skin around her chin. She airbrushed out stray pieces of hair and flecks in her irises. She erased herself.

My friends and I all watched her move through this process for a good ten minutes before we finally tuned back into the game. We kept commenting on how silly it was, and how obsessed she was, and how it was such a waste to be at a baseball game and to instead spend the time designing a perfect face to post online. It was quite sad. When I was a teenager, I had enough insecurity all on my own from just getting up in the morning and going to school. I think if I'd felt like I had to look perfect in every single picture, and then live up to that perfection when people saw me in real life, it would have been too much to take.

So many people edit their photos all the time, though, and not just teenagers or young adults. There was a woman I used to follow on Facebook who airbrushed every single picture of her face such that she looked like a porcelain doll in all of her selfies. There was another woman I knew, a dancer in her late thirties, who was obviously in good shape and was quite pretty. But I used to think of her as a peacock. She put so much colorful makeup on her face that I didn't actually know what she looked like. And she spent so much time stopping to take pictures of herself in her skimpy dance clothes, I often wondered how much she actually practiced at all.

I think of these people now and I wonder if they will ever grow out of the need to take pictures of themselves, showing what appears to be perfection. The teenager? Well, she has more time. But the adults? Will they ever find the inner confidence to post a picture with no makeup, perhaps as they are sitting around on a Sunday afternoon feeling a lot of joy because their cat made them smile?

I never used to go anywhere without makeup. And this would be a full face—foundation, powder, eye shadow, blush, eyeliner, mascara, lipstick. But when I got really sick, it all flew out the window and you'd be lucky to catch me with any makeup on at all. I think of this sequence of unfortunate events as a blessing because it helped me to let go of the insecurities I'd carried with me for so long.

I've started posting makeup-free pictures on Instagram and Facebook over the last few years. Pictures that are not very flattering, per say, but that illustrate moments I'm proud of (and that have nothing to do with my physical appearance). I've posted pictures of my success with walking down the street when I couldn't walk before. I've posted pictures of something I've been able to cook for myself in the kitchen, when I couldn't cook—or even eat—before. I've posted pictures with my husband, who hung out on the couch with me as I battled fatigue. I've cared more about showing our love than about hiding my pale skin and puffy eyes.

🍃 🍃 🍃

I think it's good to take a selfie every once in a while. We should document ourselves as we go through life, because we are lucky enough to do so. How I wish I were able to see more pictures of myself as I was growing up, or of my grandmother as she was making her way through the prime years of her life. The ability to take pictures of anything and at any time, to an unlimited degree, is such a gift that we have in our modern lives. But maybe let's go back to using the camera as a way to document our lives, our travels, and the things that make us happy rather than as a way to show off. Maybe let's look at the whole photo-taking process as our wanting to be in the picture in order to remember the feeling we had that day or the beautiful thing we saw—not because we've got to get that selfie posted to Facebook and hope it gets twenty "likes."

WHEN LIFE DOESN'T
GO AS PLANNED

On my thirty-fifth birthday, I found myself in one of those laboratories where they line you up like cattle and stick you in the arm, one person after another, and draw out your blood like a mosquito. It's an annoyance for some people and an absolute anxiety attack for others. Where do I fall on that spectrum? Well, I struggle to hold on to consciousness every single time.

This particular visit to the lab was especially frustrating because I was getting seventeen vials (yep, that's right) of blood drawn, plus I had to drink something particularly acrid and breathe into a bag about sixty seconds later, all in the name of figuring out what was wrong with me. This was the extent of what I did for my thirty-fifth birthday. I was in the midst of waiting for my gallbladder removal surgery and therefore couldn't eat a smidgen of fat (which basically means you can't eat anything), so I went home and sucked down some chicken broth and called it a night.

On my thirty-sixth birthday, I found myself unusually lonely in my long-time city. My best friend had moved away the month before and my other good friend had dropped me like a hot potato after my two surgeries. Another had bailed when I got married without giving me any explanation as to why. So my dear husband attempted to cobble together a last-minute dinner with whomever he could find, and I ended up quietly sharing a meal with two couples—one who is dear to me but who arrived exceptionally late, and another who I hardly knew but whose wife got plastered and loud, embarrassing me greatly.

I didn't want to have another birthday.

On my thirty-seventh birthday, I found myself at home on my couch, scowling at my husband's leg propped up on some pillows because he'd injured his knee in basketball three days earlier. We were supposed to be in Florida, waving hello to Mickey Mouse and subsequently collapsing onto the nearest beach. But we'd had to cancel our trip less than twelve hours before the flight. So for that birthday, I ate lunch with my husband, enjoyed a gluten-free cake that my best friend had frantically ordered from the local bakery, fed some ducks at a nearby pond, and then trekked it on home to ring in another year of my life.

Sometimes things just don't go as planned.

My own life has felt like a long string of coincidences, detours, unexpected setbacks and totally-not-what-I-thought-I'd-be-doing instances. It's been a ride I might have gotten off of had I known earlier on what was to come. And it's nothing like how I used to imagine myself as a grown-up. You know, the plans I devised for myself in my quiet moments.

I imagined dinner parties with friends where I arrived in my best clothes and laughed contentedly. I pictured a house of my own—a nice one—full of pretty things and high-quality furniture, with an exceptionally clean carpet that was nothing like the stained, fur-covered messes of my childhood. I dreamed of vacations and romance, and taking trips to the theatre (because I would be cultured and refined, of course).

But when I got to the actual grown-upness, I was underwhelmed to find my life was set in an apartment. It was one that got progressively nicer over the years, but it was still an apartment. And while I did have a few pieces of nice clothing, I never got invited to dinner parties so I rarely wore them. I didn't laugh contentedly with friends for very long, either, because they often moved away, or had kids, or changed their minds about the friendship, or shifted their priorities. I had a husband but it was after spending many years as a divorcée (that hadn't been expected, either). And while our marriage continues to be wonderful and happy most of the time, it didn't unfold like one of the romantic comedies I'd watched in my adolescence. I'd had to educate myself elsewhere about relationships since my parents had divorced when I was three years old.

❦ ❦ ❦

It's really easy to get discouraged when you examine your life and start noticing all the things that you wish weren't there. Like the job you don't really want to have, or the white wall across from your couch that you thought would contain a fireplace by now. Or maybe it's the health that ran away and doesn't want to return, or the relationship that fizzled for reasons you don't understand.

It's also easy to fall into thinking that you fatally messed up and it's too late to fix it. That you're just too old or you don't know how. And then there are bills over here, and obligations over there, and you're so tired at the end of the day that you stretch out on your sofa (which is still not across from a fireplace) until you pass into the darkness of sleep. You've missed the boat, you think, so you may as well camp out where you are.

But life always gives us chances to course correct and to create a new plan if we can get past the internal noise. The first question is, do you pay attention to the messages when they come? And after that (and this is important), do you follow through?

* * *

When I got really sick at age thirty-four and went through my two surgeries, I did what most people who'd almost expired do: I "woke up" to my mortality and was therefore determined not to waste another minute of my life. I strapped myself onto an imaginary rocket, lit the fuse, and was ready to soar. I was going to write my books and start dreaming my dreams again. I was going to stop working jobs I hated, or at least stop letting them make me so miserable that they blocked me from growing into who I was supposed to be. I felt the universe had used my health crisis to shake me out of my sleepwalking, and this time I'd just sidestep the fear and bills and rationality because … I had almost ceased to exist! What the hell had I been doing every day?

I think many life-changing experiences don't change us in the ways we'd hoped they would, or perhaps that they should. I've seen this over and over again as I've watched people come close to the edge of ruin, or even close to death, and yet still revert back to whatever destructive behavior they engaged in before. I was no different and reverted back into my old life within months, trudging along again and losing myself in the monotone existence of work and obligations. I think this happens because once you pull out of survival mode, you find yourself plopped back into the same situation you were in before—the same home, the same bills, the same family, the same obligations. Really, the same life that didn't go as planned and that also hasn't really changed despite your life-changing event. This is when rationalization takes over and dreams again fade away.

You didn't follow through. Maybe you will next time.

Just because things don't go as planned doesn't mean they aren't actually going as planned, though. Sometimes you simply don't *like* the plan until it fully unfolds and you can put on your hindsight goggles. Other times you get distracted or veer off course for a while—for years or for decades—and this is more what I'm talking about. I'm talking about those times when you find yourself gnawed by discontentment or things being "not right." Those are the times when you have to take the initiative to redirect your energy and your thoughts into the place you'd rather be.

It's never too late to get back on track if you feel like you've faltered, despite the voice inside your head that says, *you're too old* or *you've lost too much time*. You are still alive. And as long as you're alive, there is something you still need to do or to figure out. There is still time to get it right. There is still time to reinvent yourself. There is still time to become.

Personally, I take some comfort in knowing that most of us are not where we want to be. If we were, nobody would have goals or ambition or dreams. So don't beat yourself up or think it's just too late if you aren't able to do what you want to do just yet. If we quietly strive for a different reality, step-by-step and day-by-day, it's okay if the momentum is slow but the trajectory is forward. A quiet, daily striving is probably what most of humanity does anyway.

THE LAZY RIVER

I think that as the years pass by you become less afraid because you have less time left on the planet. And when you start running out of time, you start running out of fear. Fear about doing things, anyway, because the distress of *not* having done them starts to grow over everything like a rogue English ivy.

I had this experience in my late thirties as I trudged to my desk one Monday morning after a long weekend of relaxing on my couch. I'd preceded this trudging with a lot of bemoaning, blues, procrastination, and also some irritability the night before. My job was one that paid me well (which I liked) but that didn't utilize my skills or talents at all (which I didn't like). I'd coasted along for well over three years because it had served my needs for a while, and also because I didn't have the balls to call out my own unhappiness and do something about it.

And this is the thing: our experiences (jobs, relationships, challenges, heartaches) serve our needs for a time, and when the time is up we have to move on. Doing so often takes some effort, and this is where sometimes we fall short. Because change is hard. Venturing out is hard. Finding a new rhythm is hard. But not initiating a needed change can cause us to stagnate and spin in stationary circles that grow into years or decades. And if we succumb to the inertia for too long, we'll eventually wake up old and grumpy with a rearview mirror full of regrets and missed opportunities.

The problem I faced in my late thirties was that I'd been searching frantically for a way to stay happy in an unfulfilling job while pursuing my other interests, because I did really want a home of my own someday and a shot at being able to retire. I was hopeful this job was the right path to those things for me, and to be honest it *was* the right path for a while. We were able to save a cushion of money and find some financial security we hadn't experienced before. We also got to take a couple of trips that made us happy, and buy a much-needed new car with a manageable payment, because we could put some money aside instead of starting out totally in the red. Those were all good things that really needed to happen in our lives.

So I think the red flags didn't show themselves while the job was serving its purpose because I was supposed to be there at that time in my life. The key, though, was recognizing when it was time for me to step out of that scene and into a new one. And I had missed the cue. Or, I simply chose not to hear it, because I was enjoying the side effects of the job even though I wasn't happy Monday through Friday between nine and five.

🍃 🍃 🍃

Life is not about riding in a lazy river, watching the twists and turns as you idly move along. Sometimes you have to get out of the river and walk a while to avoid being carried out to sea, where you'd just join the others who have coasted along before you without having the courage to find their own way. These people didn't become part of the rest of the world, with its network of intertwined paths that crisscross and connect in certain places like tunnels on an ant farm. They weren't part of anything bigger than just the single river—the single path—from which they came.

On that Monday morning, I finally realized I was not just unhappy; I was now going in the wrong direction. I stared at my computer screen for a long time. I glanced to the side at my large day planner, with my list of To Dos in neat black ink, and I realized that I could not, for one more second, do these things. I could not, for one more week, sit there every morning checking monotonous items off a list just to get a paycheck. The paycheck was no longer enough to compensate for the misery this little list was causing me. It didn't make up for the missed opportunities, or for being pushed into a river going south instead of stepping out and moving west, or for not living a life that felt part of the larger world and therefore would mean something when I died.

I told my husband (we share an office) that I was going for a walk and I'd be back in a while. I circled around the park a few times and let my thoughts swirl up into the sky. I already knew what I needed to do, but I was afraid to do it. To quit would be taking one of those leaps people talk about, and I wasn't sure how I felt about that—especially not when I'd made so many seemingly wrong turns in my life. This was a situation I'd experienced many times before in my career, and my next role often turned into a rerun of the one I'd just left.

But sometimes you have to look at things in a broader sense. I'd thought I was doing that by staying at a job that would give me long-term financial security, but what I'd really been doing was staying at a job that had held me prisoner through fear—fear of the unknown, fear of failing, fear of making a bad decision, fear of not solving the problem. And of course, fear of unfairly burdening the person I loved (and still love) most with the task of taking care of the entire household while I laid there like a beached whale.

As I said, though, sometimes you just run out of fear because you realize you will run out of time—and that's what was happening to me during this moment in the park. I can only imagine that this scenario intensifies as you plow your way through the rest of your life and see the road ahead growing shorter. For me, approaching forty and having already lost a few years to chronic illness, I was feeling the urgency more strongly than ever. I was not going to lose another year of my life due to circumstances that I could, in fact, control.

So I put a plan in place and I committed to it. Once I did that, my next task was to become comfortable with the fear and uncertainty, since staying stuck was no longer an option. I was going to embrace my decision to resign and proceed boldly, but also with a teaspoon of faith and a swig of numbing alcohol. (Metaphorically speaking, of course. But any change is really hard.)

🌿 🌿 🌿

I don't know as of this writing how things will turn out for me, but if you're reading these words then I can say they turned out exactly how I wished they would, and how I think they were supposed to. I'd wanted to do more meaningful work for a long time, but I was shriveling up in a corner, beaten down by the pummeling of busy work.

And what would have happened if I'd succumbed to my fears? Chased the green? Laid down with my financial security in an inner tube and drifted down the river? Maybe I would have gotten my house and secured my retirement while somehow managing to tolerate my days. More likely I would have been cut anyway, because a few months later, I heard they let my replacement go due to a change in direction.

Luckily I didn't stay around to find out. I jumped onto the rocks and ran in the other direction.

THE MORNING AFTER

This is not an essay about sex. Although I suppose it *could* be an essay about sex, but I've never had a one-night stand so I don't know what that feels like the morning after (I imagine not all that great?). This is an essay about how your feelings or thoughts about something often change the morning after. I've found that this waking-up experience can be positive or negative, depending on what happened the day before.

Maybe you had an all-out fist fight (metaphorically) with your spouse and you both just decided to end in a draw, go to sleep, and see how you felt in the morning. Maybe you were feeling like a garbage truck hit you (physically or emotionally) and you decided the best thing to do was to close your eyes to the world, turn off your brain, and start the next day fresh. Or on the flip side, maybe you'd made a hugely impactful life decision that you felt good about making, so you went to sleep happy and at peace but then woke up the next day to a mind spinning with doubt.

I think we often choose our daily actions based on either a gut reaction or an impulse. Other times we act based on logic. For example, it's a gut reaction when you throw your abusive boyfriend out the door for the last time, because after he pinned you down and tried to punch you in the face, you decided enough was enough (yes, that was when I finally left him). It's an impulse when you go to the mall with the intent to purchase everything you like, whether or not you can actually pay for it, because there are credit cards for that and you feel like stuffing your face with donuts soaked in wine anyway (maybe you'll pick those up too, while you're at it). It's logic when you are deciding between restaurants for your weekly date night and you choose the one that fits properly within your budget constraints.

These are the day-to-day life decisions that precede our morning afters. And I think most of the time, one of two things happens when we wake up the next day: either our brain turns on to try to talk us out of something good that we already decided upon, or our gut turns on to tell us what we did the day before was maybe not the best idea.

🌣 🌣 🌣

Now for me, I'm not one to succumb to shopping impulses or random shouting matches—although it did feel empowering to stand on a table and yell at a privileged, suit-wearing white dude in my dream last night. But I *am* one to talk myself out of decisions that I know are good for me, sometimes for months or for years, because I'm afraid of the unknown. And on the flip side, I'm also one to wake up the day after finally listening to my gut, or sometimes a few days later if I'm riding a wave of excitement or relief, and then try to logically talk myself out of whatever it was I finally did. If I'm not careful, this voice that comes around on the second day can totally derail the plans I need to be making and the decisions I need to be implementing in my life. So I've learned that the morning-after mental chatter is usually something to ignore.

Now I would say the opposite is true for things like spats, depressed ruminations, stubbing my toe and then hitting my knee on the coffee table, or messing up dinner. These are events that resolve themselves by the time I get to the morning after, and I do like to pay attention to the lightness in my head when I wake up. In fact, as I've gotten older, I've learned that sleep can be a magical sponge that washes away the grime of the day so you can start shiny and new again tomorrow. Have you ever woken up after a particularly harrowing day and felt like, suddenly, life is not so harrowing anymore? And it's just because you woke up to a new sunrise—not because anything actually changed. That's the magic of sleep.

With all of that said, I know going to sleep (and staying there) is the epitome of what a depressed person wants to do. Well, that or drowning their sorrows in a bottle. But sometimes going to sleep is actually just the fix for whatever seemed to be going wrong in your life that day. And not a nap, that doesn't work. You have to sleep overnight to give your subconscious time to detach and find its way back to a peaceful place.

There are many nights when I wake up a lot. And sometimes I'll wake up and remember the thing that I was running away from by sleeping, and I'll feel the dread welling up in my body and slowly making its way to my brain. But then I'll tell myself, *Just go back to sleep. You'll feel better in the morning.*

Sleep can be such a transformative experience that really serves as a wall between not just our days, but also our thoughts, feelings, and life chapters. I think it allows our guts to kick in—or maybe our souls—and that process reminds our subconscious that whatever happened is really not such a big deal as long as nobody is dead or dismembered. To wake up alive and experience another day is actually a big deal. To wake up healthy is a big deal. To wake up in a warm home or in a home filled with love is a big deal. And maybe that thing you were so worried about yesterday just doesn't matter at all.

SOME PEOPLE HAVE IT HARDER THAN OTHERS

*A*s much as we'd all like to think the world is an equitable place if you work hard enough, in my experience it's just not. This is easier to see when you look at impoverished countries and people who bury their babies due to starvation. I think most of us pause when we're confronted with those images, and we ponder (consciously or not) why we were born into different circumstances. But it's sometimes harder to see it in our day-to-day lives, when we go to work and are surrounded by people who seemingly have the same circumstances or motivations as we do. The inequality just isn't always so obvious if you have a small sphere of friends or are sitting near the top of the income brackets.

One of my biggest pet peeves is the "pull yourself up by your bootstraps" mentality. It's an idea that is really pervasive in my particular culture (here in the United States) and also in my family. Maybe this concept functioned better when we had a robust middle class, lots of land for the taking, jobs that paid a living wage, and affordable college tuition. But I suspect there were just better odds back then; I'm not convinced this idea was ever a life truth.

The bootstraps idea is that we are all on a level playing field and that if you just play the game smarter, or harder, you'll score the points and win at life. There are many people who believe this is the case, and that's okay. We are all allowed to believe whatever we want. I also know, though, that there is a large segment of the population who feels like sometimes it doesn't *matter* how hard you play or how smart you are; sometimes you just can't win the game, and it doesn't have anything to do with where you came from or what sort of education you have.

Sometimes life just isn't fair.

⊘ ⊘ ⊘

Until I took that trip to Hawaii at age thirty, after I'd left my teaching job, I'd thought my life was the epitome of struggle and bad luck. However, as I got older and met more people, heard more stories, and read more of the news, I started to change my thought processes. I didn't feel quite so sorry for myself anymore, although there were definitely a lot of things I could have felt sorry for myself about. I learned that I didn't have a monopoly on heartbreak, or poverty, or unemployment, or health problems. And, in fact, sometimes the stories I heard from others were worse than my own stories. It was quite the revelation when I'd lived my entire life thinking mine was the worst.

Still, there was a pesky nagging when I looked around me at the people who shared some of my circumstances but somehow seemed happier and more successful than I was. I'd gone to college just like they did. I'd worked hard in my jobs. I'd tried to be a good person and to do good to others. I'd never done drugs or cheated on tests or purposely disrespected my parents. And for most of my life, I'd followed all of the rules of the Bible like it was a playbook for success, except that I hadn't achieved the type of success I thought would be promised to me.

Maybe I'd misinterpreted the text.

Somehow I'd found myself cheated on (and subsequently divorced), jobless (and subsequently penniless), suicidal (more than once), and apartment-less (and therefore shut up in a small room with my two cats and a couple of suitcases). So many negative things had befallen me for so many years from my teens to my late-thirties, despite feeling like I'd followed all of the rules, that I'd spent a good part of that time trying to figure out why life seemed to come easier for some people and not for others.

Now I will say that a large part of my problem was perception. We all generally perceive others to have happier and more fulfilling lives than we do, and probably than they *actually* do themselves. But the other thing I've noticed is that sometimes you just don't get lucky. Sometimes tragedy befalls you. Sometimes shit hits the fan. Sometimes bad things happen to good people.

I could think of a million analogies or sayings to describe what we all see as the unfairness of life, and there's a reason people have constructed these sayings: humans realized long ago that unfairness seemed to be a life truth. But even so, there are those humans who skirt the obvious and like to assign blame, claiming that maybe not everyone tries hard enough or puts in the work. I'm sure this is true sometimes, but I've met so many people who try really hard at life and still can't achieve success.

❦ ❦ ❦

As I've gone through my own struggles, I've learned to become a more compassionate human being. I've also learned I've got a stubborn blemish inside of me that manifests in the form of jealousy or bitterness, because there are things in life that I wish would have happened but didn't (or that happened and I wish hadn't). And of course, I often look around and am convinced everyone else has a more positive outlook and journey through life. (My logical brain knows this isn't the case, though.)

And that's my point, I suppose. We all seem to have those feelings of inadequacy and we all seem to compare ourselves to others. So we need to be open to the idea that things are not always in our control and that unfairness is a part of life we have to accept. It's so easy for me, personally, to fall into bad patterns of thinking—especially when life isn't going my way. But these days I try to remind myself of my personal belief that everything happens for a reason—and that some people do have it harder than others.

Perhaps it's because there is an ultimate playbook in the sky and we are all only a small part of it. Opening your mind to this playbook concept doesn't have to mean you believe in anything specific. Maybe you think all of nature is interconnected and you are a part of that. Maybe you believe in a higher power whose hand is in everything we experience, or maybe you don't buy into any of this stuff at all. And that's okay.

I just hope that as a collective consciousness, and because all of us have the capacity to effect positive or negative change, we can strive toward compassion before judgment. We can realize we all have unique circumstances and challenges, and that failure or downtrodden circumstances are not always the consequences of poor decisions (although, sure, they are sometimes). Sometimes people have done everything right, or they've done everything you would have done, and things still don't go their way.

Maybe it's just not their fault.

JUMP OFF THE
BANDWAGON

There are a lot of things in this world that just don't work for me but seem to work for everyone else—violent movies, McMansions, super-sugary root beer, binge-watching television shows. As one of my most glaring personal examples of a bandwagon I can't seem to stay on, I'm unable to make meditation stick. And for normal people this isn't a big deal. But for me, it's troublesome because I'm a certified yoga teacher who is also certified to teach meditation. It's a common thread that stitches all of the yoga teachers I know (except myself) into a line.

One of the first questions the instructors would ask each weekend of my nine-month training program was, "So how is your meditation practice?" I tried for many years to meditate, mostly because my yoga training encouraged me to do so. But I also did it because I thought it was the secret key to life that only a few had been able to discover. I thought maybe it was the thing to finally help me find peace and an ability to cope with stress, instead of just playing dodgeball with my troubles every day.

But after several years of trying, the longest I've been able to do it consistently is a couple of months. Granted, I felt more grounded and centered and peaceful in those couple of months than I usually did. I also came to enjoy the quiet and to really like the practice, although I couldn't sustain it for more than fifteen minutes per session ("they" say I need to do more). So I *do* recognize how much it could help me if only I could stick with it.

Meanwhile, the magazines of mainstream America have decided meditation is the newest fad. I'm reading about it from the usual suspects, like spiritual advisors and yoga teachers, and also from doctors, scientists, and psychologists. What more evidence do I need that this is something I should be doing every day? So, time and again, I buckle down and try even harder to do this thing that just doesn't come naturally to me, and that oftentimes causes me more anxiety than not.

🍃 🍃 🍃

Somewhere along the line I decided it's okay to jump off a bandwagon. I used to feel like a failure if I couldn't do something that seemed awfully easy to the rest of humanity, or that was prescribed as necessary by those in positions to make such decisions. But I now realize we are all unique and that prescribing a single set of rules for getting through life just doesn't work. Dieting? Forget it. Spin classes? No thanks. Finding a church home? Doesn't feel right. Climbing the corporate ladder? *Misery.*

I think the idea of doing what works best for us (and ignoring the rest) should be integrated into everything we do and into all of the choices we make as we go through life. So many of us try to do what everyone else does, or what they say we should do, so we can fit in and feel like we've somehow walked along a successful life path. We buy houses, sometimes bigger than we need. We trade in cars, even when the ones we have are just fine. We get more clothes, despite our closet doors barely staying shut. And then we stay in jobs that turn us into machines so we can support all of these activities.

That's not to say getting a house or a car or new clothes is bad. I think it's only bad if you're doing it to feel like you're accomplished enough to sit at the collective table. I think it's also bad if you're falling victim to the "less than" mentality and perceive your friends as having made it to some level you still strive to reach. But if you've been driving a clunker for a while, why not buy a new car? Do you have the money? Does it make you happy? Sure, go for it.

The beauty of life, if we learn to see it, is that we can try to make it into something that perfectly suits us—if we can let go of the need to compete, that is. We can really ask ourselves, *What makes me happy? Where do I thrive?* And we can go and try to do those things. This is not to say life is easy; a lot of times we know what will make us happy although we just can't attain it. Not yet. But at least we can go in the general direction of bliss and maybe we'll get there one day.

As for me? I no longer try to meditate unless I just feel like it, and I do sometimes. Every few months I'll wake up in the morning, decide I want to find some stillness, and pull out my unworn meditation cushion for a little while. And I'm always glad I did. The difference now is that I no longer scold myself for not doing it more often, or for not doing it longer, or for not doing it every day like a good yogi should (because that's what us yogis are supposed to do, if we are real ones, anyway). It's about the inner journey, so they say.

Well my inner journey likes to take a detour around meditation and into other things like gardening, cooking, writing, walking, or spending time with my cats. And this is okay too. It's all okay. In fact, the bandwagon is a human construct that doesn't really exist. It's one of those ideas dreamed up to help keep us all in line and going down a certain path (one that is usually healthy and good, but that's beside the point). If riding the bandwagon does that for you, that's great! That's what it was designed to do. But if it makes you feel miserable? Get out and walk down your own path on foot. There are no real rules here except to play nice as you move along.

CLEANING THE BATHROOM

When I was in my second year of college, I found myself working at one of those pizza and game places that caters to young children. Now this place really is lovely if you are a kid. It's a wonderland of animated robots and video games and, at least back in the eighties, ball pits you could burrow into and hide from your parents. This was perhaps the most fun part of all.

I was twenty years old and studying for my English degree when I ended up working part-time there as a way to make ends meet. I didn't set my goals on spending my entire weekend at this mini amusement park for kids. In fact, I've never been much of a kid person, but mostly because I never had any around. I ended up in this job because I'd found myself suddenly unemployed the day after Christmas. I was sitting on the couch in my grandmother's living room, watching the news on her old console TV, and a headline blasted across the bottom of the screen stating that Montgomery Ward was going out of business.

"Oh," I said, "I guess I'm out of a job?"

Thanks, corporate America.

I'd continued to work at Montgomery Ward as long as they let me, clearing out the store like a street sweeper and watching people carry the merchandise away like ants. This lasted maybe two months and then I found myself sitting in my sixth-floor dorm room, unemployed, charging new tires and the occasional grocery item to my credit card while wondering what the hell I was going to do for money.

When you're in a small-ish town—and especially a college town—it's rather hard to find a job when there are so many other people doing exactly that. So, if you're lucky enough to get one, you hold on to it no matter how ill-suited it might be to your personality. As much as I hated that job at the pizza place (it goes down in my personal history as my worst job of all time), I clung to it as long as I could stand it. In fact, I would have stayed longer except my then-boyfriend was in basic training and got a weekend furlough two hours away. When they refused to let me off work to see him (I hadn't seen him in six months and I was young and in love), I walked out the door and decided to deal with the fallout later.

Now, before I get sued for libel by the kids' pizza place executives, there is nothing inherently wrong with establishments like that. When I was raising my stepson in my early twenties, I took him there quite often so he could Tasmanian Devil his way through the place and then provide me with some peace and quiet afterward. But when I worked there as a twenty-year-old, I had to do all sorts of vomit-inducing tasks like cleaning up food projectiles and wiping down spit. I also was subjected to kids screaming all day long to a background track of Beach Boys songs on repeat, which mangled my eardrums and beat the joy out of my soul.

But by far the worst part of that job was cleaning the bathrooms. If you haven't cleaned a public bathroom, congratulations! You've missed out on possibly one of the grossest aspects of life there is (although perhaps performing emergency bowel surgery would be worse). I would prefer not to go into detail about the things I had to look at and clean, but suffice it to say there were toilets to be unclogged, urinals that were no longer white, and sinks that were covered in brown.

Luckily for me, my tenure was only a few months before I walked out. I was able to move on to a new job at a retail shop in the mall. However, I realized at that young age that there are people in this world who still have to clean those bathrooms. For years. For their entire lives.

These are bathrooms you and I use and scrutinize when we're at the local café, or when we need to make a pit stop during our grocery shopping. Then there are the ones we step out of meetings to visit in our office buildings, or that we stop to use after church before heading to brunch. We often forget that these places don't function by themselves when hundreds of (sometimes careless) people stop into them all the time.

There are a lot of people in the world who really believe they are above such a thing as cleaning bathrooms, but the reality is nobody is above anything.

Nobody is better than or less than. These are all societal and class constructs we've invented to create feelings of accomplishment and achievement—i.e., I got an education so I could advance into *this* job and not stay "low" like a janitor.

If we could somehow take all the job labels off and just look at one another as fellow humans, we would see that we are all exactly the same. We all feel happiness and sadness, wake up and go to sleep, get hungry and thirsty, feel love and sometimes hatred. The woman who cleans your bathroom could easily be you, and you could easily be her, perhaps if circumstances were different or if the dominos had fallen in a different direction.

So if you find yourself cleaning a bathroom, know that some of us realize the truth—that you are just as essential to the world as any other person in it. Your job matters just as much as mine because what you do directly impacts me. Thank you for cleaning the bathroom.

If you find yourself disdaining people who clean bathrooms, ask yourself why you do so. Is it because you feel superior? Is it because you feel separate? Maybe it's because you're afraid to look at someone who has a different life than you do?

I'm happy I had the opportunity to clean bathrooms because I now understand what it feels like to clean up the messes of other humans like a broken record. I've grown more empathetic to people, and I've also learned to say "hello" to the women who work tirelessly (and usually silently) in those rooms.

Don't ever assume any job is beneath you. You never know which way the world will turn because that is the way of the world, and your future work situation isn't written in stone. We see these shifts time and again with cycles of war and poverty and unrest, as stability evaporates and job opportunities diminish.

If you woke up one day as a janitor, simply because it's the way things worked out, you sure would want people to see you for you, right?

PREJUDICE LIVES
WITHIN US ALL

I was in my local natural grocer the other day picking up a few things. You know, the essentials like bananas and my favorite frozen veggie burgers. It was the middle of the day and therefore the number of cashiers was low, so I went to the one checkout lane that was open for "10 items or less." I moved closer only to find a cashier ringing up a thin, attractive woman with wavy blonde hair—one who probably had double the amount of allowed items in her basket, and who couldn't seem to make up her mind about what she was actually buying. She'd grabbed an armful of supplement bottles along with a small tub of yogurt and, as each one was scanned, she seemed to question her decision to purchase each one, reaching over the computer screen to re-examine the items just to be sure.

I was too far away to hear the conversation between the two of them so I created some dialogue for them in my brain. We don't do this consciously, of course, but I think many of us ascribe thoughts and words to people who annoy us but whom we can't actually hear or tell off. I imagined it went something like this based on what I observed:

Customer: Do you know what this is for?

Cashier: No, I'm sorry.

Customer: How much is it again?

Cashier: $13.99

Customer: I think I have two of these, hold on let me look. Can I see the basket?

Cashier: <blank stare; hands over basket>

Customer: Oh, yes, I do. I don't want both of those, I only want one.

Cashier: Okay.

Customer: Oh, how much is this one?

Cashier: $8.99

Customer: Oh! Did I have any more of those in my basket?

Cashier: Umm. I'm not sure ....

Customer: Can I look in the bag to check?

Cashier, handing over the bagged items: Okay.

Customer: No, I don't have another one. Let me run back and get another bottle.

Cashier: O ... kay ....

At this point she did run away, mumbling a quick "Sorry!" in my direction, and about thirty seconds later, she returned with a bottle of something that replaced another bottle of something that she told the cashier to set aside. She then asked to look in the shopping bag again, rummaged around, asked another question, decided all was okay, and proceeded to insert her credit card.

Geez, I said to myself. *Calm down, Elizabeth, you aren't in a rush. Be patient. No need to get irritable. She's almost done.*

But no, the checkout process didn't go smoothly either. She didn't remove her card when it started beeping and she again asked the cashier more questions. And even when she finally grabbed the bag to walk away, she still wasn't done asking questions. How many questions could she *possibly* have? I was running out of ones to imagine.

I started unloading my six items onto a counter that was now, annoyingly, cluttered with her unwanted purchases. I then did something I hadn't done until that point in my observation: I gave her a label. And what I mean is, I decided she wasn't quite "there" and that maybe she also lacked a bit in intelligence. She smiled at me and I half smiled back, and then she finally took off hurriedly to the exit.

I thought this would be the end of things, of course. I completed my purchase rather uneventfully and marched out into the cold air with my reusable bag. And then I saw her, walking one way down the middle of the street, and then the other, not really paying attention to traffic and looking rather discombobulated. I shook my head disapprovingly, glanced toward my car, and kept walking. I was almost there when I heard a faint, "Excuse me!" and I thought to myself, *Bah!*

Of course I turned around, because although I'd labeled her as "weird" and a "little off" while inside the store, I am not a rude or hateful person in general. I looked directly at her, wondering if she was talking to me (she was) and what she needed now (hadn't she asked enough questions inside?).

"Excuse me, can you help me?" she asked. "Do you know where Walmart is?"

I met her gaze and saw a twinkle in her eye and the nicest smile, and she had a very slight accent I couldn't place. It was then that my annoyance melted and I realized what an ass I'd been. I was only an ass in my own thoughts, of course, which I suppose is commendable as compared to some humans who spew their internal negativity boldly and in broad daylight.

"Yes, it's that way. But it's a long way to walk. Are you trying to walk there?"

"Yes, I'm staying at that hotel over there," she said, pointing, "and I was going to walk over after I got done here."

"Oh, well it's not very far but you probably don't want to walk. Traffic is getting heavy and it would take you a little while to get over there. Why don't I just take you?"

"Are you sure?" She cracked a smile.

"Yes I'm sure. It's no problem at all." I smiled back.

"Are you sure you don't mind? Really? That's so nice of you. Are you sure?"

"Yes, of course. Just come on this way and we'll go. It won't take long."

"Wow, thank you so much."

We walked the remaining distance to my tiny little Civic coupe, and I dumped my bag into the trunk so she would have room in the front seat. My car was clean but dusty, and needed a good vacuuming along the floor, but not too shabby overall for being more than five years old. She slid in, closed the door, and fastened the seat belt tightly against her small frame.

"My car is little but it does the job," I smiled at her. She smiled back.

"Thank you so much," she said. "There really are nice people still left in the world." I paused. Her words hit my heart and it thumped hard.

"Well, I like to think there are," I said to her, in all seriousness because I'd been thinking about it a lot lately, "but sometimes it sure feels like there aren't."

She didn't say anything for a moment, and then resumed.

"I'm not in town for very long."

"Oh? Where are you from?"

"Europe. I'm a flight attendant."

"Oh. Well, welcome to our country! I'm sorry things are so bad right now," I apologized rather solemnly. We were a few years into the Trump administration, and a wide cloud of darkness seemed to have settled over everything.

"Well, it's not you."

"That's true."

I looked ahead at the cars on the road, thinking about how the people of Russia don't equal their leader, either. And how nobody *I* know wants to lock kids up in cages. Or pardon people convicted of war crimes. Or rub shoulders with dictators. Or alienate all of our allies.

"What's your name?" she asked.

"My name's Elizabeth. What's yours?"

"Sofia."

"Nice to meet you," I said, perking up.

"So nice to meet you!"

We drove out of the parking lot and around a turn to get onto the busy street.

"Walmart is right over there," I said, pointing, "You see why it's best not to walk? This is a busy intersection and it's still a ways over that way."

"Oh, yes, I see."

"Where in Europe are you from?" I asked.

"I'm from Germany."

"Oh, that's nice. My husband went there once." We turned the corner and started down a smaller street toward Walmart.

"You should come sometime! If you're ever in Europe, I'll show you around! Oh, I just love it there."

I laughed, thinking of how expensive a trip like that usually is.

"If I can get to Europe, that would be nice!" I said.

We pulled into the parking lot and I started playing dodgeball with cars. Everyone in a rush: it's the American way.

"Well, where would you like me to drop you off?" I asked. "Groceries or the home section?"

"Oh, it doesn't matter, you can drop me anywhere." She started to undo her seat belt while I was in the middle of the parking lot and still driving. The beeping made her quickly re-engage it.

"Okay, how about I drop you off over by that door?" I asked and nodded toward the home entrance.

"Sure. Thank you so much! This was just so nice of you."

"Not a problem at all. I live right down the street so it was on my way."

We smiled at each other.

Sofia was a nice woman. She was smart. She was kind. She was not "weird" or "off" or "slow." She was just a foreigner who was out of her element and approaching the world like a wide-eyed child—just as I do when I'm in a foreign place. *Oh, Elizabeth.*

"Here you are."

I put my car in park and turned on my flashers. I noticed a few nasty glares out of the corner of my eye. It was December, after all. Not the time to dilly-dally in front of the Walmart entrance.

She started to get out and then stopped. "Would you like to exchange emails?" she asked. I was so glad she did, because in that moment I was wishing for more.

"Yes, I would! Let me find something to write on and a pen."

I rummaged around in my glove compartment and came up with a half-working, half-frozen pen and an old, crumpled receipt. She scribbled her email address down and handed it over. We smiled again at each other, and I knew I'd probably never see her again. I suspect she realized the same. And I was sad about that. Sometimes it's nice to share a moment in time with someone and recognize that it's just a moment. But it's one that's special because just the two of you have it lodged in your memories from now until whenever your memories stop. If they ever do.

"I'll send you an email as soon as I get home," I said.

And I did.

🍃 🍃 🍃

I have often been aware of my own prejudices because I know I have them, despite being in an interracial marriage and considering myself very open and accepting. The problem is that prejudices sneak up on you. And even if we work hard to discharge these sorts of thoughts, some of them are deeply ingrained in our psyches. They come out at inopportune times when we're impatient or annoyed or moody, or maybe just having an off day and something rubs us the wrong way.

The question I would like to ask all humans who are trying, continuously, to improve in the hopes of making the world a better place, is whether or not we can be humble enough to admit when we've gone wrong. Are we insightful enough to examine our innate prejudices and judgments? Are we bold enough to admit when we think or act in ways that we condemn others for doing? And are we soft enough to forgive ourselves, and others, when we just don't measure up to high standards?

I think back on this interaction now and I feel a number of things. Annoyed with myself is one. How could I so easily label a person as unintelligent or mentally "off"? Somebody I didn't even know? Appreciative is another. I'm grateful for the lesson the universe brought me that day to soften my heart, especially as I am confronted daily with the hatred and intolerance of our times. It was helpful for me to see that the negativity others possess still lives in me as well. But I think, most days, I have more awareness of that negativity simply due to practice.

I also feel a wistful sort of emotion when I think about that day. I liked Sofia. She would have been fun to be friends with and I think we would have had a sort of sisterhood. She had a sparkle about her that made me feel like I'd met her before, like she was everyone's friend.

In my email, I told her it was nice to meet her and I also offered up any assistance while she was in town. Later that night, I got a response: she was leaving the next morning, but she wished me well and told me to take care of myself and to keep in touch.

I do hope I see her again one day, despite that wish sounding like a pipe dream, because perhaps she'll come back to town on a layover. And if I do, next time I'll see her for who she really is: someone just like me. Like all of us. With the same light in her soul that we all possess underneath the clutter and dings and scars.

THE GOLD STAR

*W*hen we're going through things that make us upset, that hurt us, or that don't make sense, it's really easy to get angry and bitter—sometimes at the entire world. Although maybe I just speak for myself? I've had so many moments when I couldn't do that tongue in cheek "look on the bright side" or "the glass is half-full" bullshit. I mean, when you're going through the worst of the worst, sometimes those sayings are deeply infuriating and feel hopelessly naïve.

So I've tried really hard the last few years to find the lesson in whatever is happening to me. For starters, finding a lesson functions as ammo against the idea that the universe is in conspiracy against me and wants to see me tumble from grace. But the practice also helps me to grasp at an explanation when things seem totally unexplainable, which is like a balm on my wound. Because I think most of us want to know "why" when something bad happens or when we suffer greatly in life.

I've learned, though, that there may not always be a "why" in the moment or even a few years down the road. Sometimes clarity comes much later, and sometimes it doesn't seem to come at all. So I wonder if sometimes we just don't understand everything until a far later date—so far away that it's after we've already expired and are somewhere else in the ether. Anyway, repeating this hypothesis to myself feels better than not having any sort of explanation at all.

☙ ☙ ☙

One of the things in my life that's hurt the most personally has to do with the inaccessibility and inequality of health care in the United States. And I'm not going to be political here; I'm just using health care as an example because it's something that has affected me on a deeply personal level and has caused me to feel targeted by bad luck. Health care (and my inability to access it) has magnified the inherent unfairness and selfishness of the world and focused it like a bullseye on my head. I've spent tens of thousands of dollars on medical costs that I didn't get to use toward saving for a home of my own. I've screamed with vitriol at not being able to access prescriptions I need that cost more than our household's total combined monthly income. I've curled up in despair and hopelessness, thinking, *The best years of my life are over and there is nowhere to go but down,* simply because I couldn't access the treatments I need to live well.

When I was in the midst of that particular emotional tornado, I couldn't see anything but the spinning wind. The anger. The frustration. The violent feelings of hatred and unfairness that were swirling inside my being. But after my husband reached in like he always does, and yanked me out of the storm, I was able to sit quietly at a distance and think about why this might be happening to me. Why did I, Elizabeth, happen to be someone who happened to need a very expensive medication and who also happened to have the worst insurance in the world, which coincidentally also happened to have a new ten thousand-dollar lifetime cap on certain benefits? Why did that happen to me? To *me,* in particular?

The easy thing to do when presented with these types of situations is to say, "Well it's because I'm cursed!" "Because I'm unlucky." "Because everything bad happens to me and this is just another one of those things." And to be honest, I still think that way sometimes when I'm in the heat of a moment, because emotions are powerful little bombs that amputate our rational thought. But afterward, when the storm passes and I'm left with the wreckage of that experience, I can start picking up the pieces of my mind and my heart. I can look at them, one at a time, examining what the fractures really mean and how I will put them all back together again.

And this is where I try to find the aforementioned lesson.

 🍃 🍃 🍃

It's been said that things will keep happening to you on repeat until they teach you what you need to know. And based on the repetitive nonsense I've experienced in my life, I would say this is true *and* I'm a terrible learner. Sometimes I think the lesson for me with the health-care debacle is, once again, about relinquishing control.

It's a lesson in understanding that the things I can't change are the things I can't change, and that losing my inner peace for a few hours (or a few days) over something I have zero power to alter is a huge waste of my time. But other times I think I'm supposed to take those escalating feelings and channel them somewhere more productive than crying into a pillow or staring at the wall in a depressed fog. You know, like finding somewhere to share my story so that maybe someone who has the power to change whatever thing I find awful can actually work to make that change.

And that's what I'm doing as I write these words— sharing my story.

I think the entire world is like a set of dominos, and humans are all connected to one another based on our actions, our mindsets, our ability to give and receive love, and our overall attitudes. Positive attitudes can be infectious, as can laughter. A poor decision, on the other hand, will not only affect you, but it can knock down everyone around you and perhaps the people they know as well.

My goal now is to figure out what sort of domino I'm supposed to be and which direction I'm supposed to fall. If I just stew in anger, then I'm a domino spinning in place … which is rather pointless. I'm not effecting any change or using what has happened to me to create positive ripple effects. And isn't that a huge waste of time?

Lessons come in all sorts of experiences, I think, and really the best lessons seem to be learned when things don't go our way. None of us is perfect in every aspect of life, so it's sort of like being in grade school again.

We do well sometimes if we have a natural aptitude and we fail sometimes if we don't, but we're learning all the same with every new subject we encounter.

I'm not saying this is a perfect system or a perfect way to look at life. If it were, I wouldn't be writing about it because we'd all have it figured out. But I know that, for me, I see life's catastrophes a little more clearly now than I did when I was younger. Everything that happens to me is no longer slapped with a "cursed" or a "bad luck" sticker. Well, *some* things are because I think it's human nature (or maybe it's just my nature). But mostly I sit back once I've entered a more reasonable emotional state, and I ask what I can do with what's in front of me or with what just happened to me. And I look inward— at the lessons I'm struggling to learn, at the lessons I don't seem to want to learn, and at the lessons I don't yet have the capacity to learn.

Then when something finally goes away that has been occurring on repeat for many years—like when I married my wonderful husband after a string of bad and sometimes abusive relationships, or when I stopped labeling myself as a "failure" just because I failed at something I tried to do—I pat myself on the back for a job well done. A life lesson learned. Rogue emotions conquered.

Gold star for me.

WHAT TIME IS IT?

*A*s a lifelong insomniac, I'm used to waking up in the middle of the night although it's obviously not in a gleeful rapture. For many years the first thing I'd do was lift my head and turn it toward my ticking, old-school clock. And then I'd slam it back down as the voices in my brain crept in to overtake my consciousness. How many hours did I have left to sleep until I had to get up for work? And how many of those hours would it take me to actually fall asleep? Doing math in the wee hours of life is not on my list of fun things to do either.

☙ ☙ ☙

A few years ago, I decided to turn my clock around so it faced my lamp—probably after reading a random article in a magazine about improving sleep. I remember having the thought to do so, getting up from the sofa, making a beeline for the nightstand, turning the clock around with an audible scrape on the wood, and walking back out like a boss. Now you could say the more logical thing to do would have been to just get rid of the clock entirely, which I could have done (I think it cost me ten dollars). But the real reason I still have it sitting there, despite its lack of actual functionality when it's facing the lamp, is because I like the sound of the ticking. It reminds me of the clock in my grandmother's guest bedroom, where I spent a good portion of my childhood and young adulthood. I used to fall asleep to her clock and wake up to it, sometimes peering through foggy eyes to see her smiling face peeking through the crack in the door in the low morning light. Other than this rogue sentimentality that I decided is as valid for me as is my sleeping with a stuffed cat every night since a beloved kitty died, yes, my clock is generally useless and has no reason for existing in my life.

I had two goals in mind when I turned that clock around. The first was to eliminate math (okay, I joke, let's start over). The first was to eliminate anxiety about time by eliminating the thing that measures time, and the second was to improve my ability to get back to sleep by creating a scenario where I could lie to myself about what time it actually was. This strategy works pretty well because when it's dark, unless you're tracking the path of the constellations like a sailor, dark is dark is *dark*. So it's pretty much impossible to know what time it is if you just look casually out the window at the space between you and the backyard fence. The only clues to time in the nighttime space are when the last light of the sun holds the twilight, or when the first rays of morning just barely tint the sky. And neither of these moments are my problem times.

Initially, I was resistant to the idea of just letting nighttime be nighttime. Isn't measuring time what we humans like to do? We have watches, and cell phones, and clocks on our walls, and clocks on our computers, and clocks in our cars. We like to measure time so that we know where we are in the process, during our days but also during decades and lifetimes. Are we losing time? Did we waste time? How much time do we have left?

But now I think it's nice to just let go of time sometimes, like at night when I don't really need this information. And I wonder now if there are other moments in life when it would be better if I didn't know what time it was. There are already experiences in life where time naturally fades away, and aren't those the best moments? When we're deep in conversation, for example. When we're watching our kids in a play. When we're looking at the snow fall. When we're hugging someone we love. When we're painting or writing or listening to music.

And then there are experiences where we measure time obsessively. Like when we're waiting for surgery, or when we're counting down to vacation, or when we're late to a meeting, or when our loved one is scheduled to fly home. Sometimes this is helpful and sometimes it isn't. I mean, really, how much time do we actually end up wasting because of thinking about time? Especially when we worry about something that might happen later, or think about an upcoming situation that hasn't even entered into time yet.

Time does not always need to be measured, contrary to what we humans have decided over the course of history. It's important to maintain a general awareness, I think, because we have appointments to keep and obligations to meet. But maybe it's okay to let go of time once in a while, especially if you find that having the information is more detrimental than not having it.

Like when you can't fall back asleep at night.

Clearly I'm human, because sometimes my nights are still stressful and I do fret over minutes and hours. But more often than not, instead of worrying about the clock, I tell myself I'm just going to rest and be content with the act of resting. Or I get up and read a book or a magazine with my eyes purposely averted from any of the multiple timepieces in my home. And then I enjoy reading during this space that is night, a space that I have chosen not to measure, and eventually I go back to sleep.

This is not foolproof, of course, because sometimes I cheat. Case in point: occasionally, instead of turning the clock around (which is forbidden according to what I've decided), I switch my cell phone on to sneak my way around my self-imposed limitation. I don't do this often—maybe once a month—but I do it.

Ah, well. Progress is important and at least I've made progress. I'm getting it, even if I don't have it down perfectly yet. Humans are silly little creatures, aren't we? We always like to shoot ourselves in the foot.

I LOST MY HAIR

*I*n my thirties, I lost my hair. Twice. The first time it grew back almost to the thickness it had been before and for most of my life (lush and full). The second time ... well the second time was something different altogether.

       🍃 🍃 🍃

Growing up, I was the girl with the super long hair all the way down to her lower back. It was thick and wavy although fine in texture, which seemed like an oxymoron. One time a hairdresser explained (to my questioning adolescent face) that my hair could be both thick and fine at the same time. Mind blown, as the kids say.

I used to twirl my hair into thick ballet buns encased in beautiful white netting, which was held into place by black bobby pins. Sometimes in the oppressive Texas heat, my mother would gather it into a brown banana clip and let it fall where it may, up and away from my shoulders and my face. Other times, as we sat in the cool of her bedroom with the white fan whirring from the corner and the thick shades drawn to keep out the heat, she would practice her French braiding until she'd created a finished pattern that made me feel elegant and lady-like.

In the summers of my adolescence and young adulthood, I was what you might say "challenged" in the art of hairstyling. I regularly pulled it up into a scrunchie on top of my head and usually way up high near the crown (although in one particular decade, I wore it sort of cockeyed to the side; it went well with my mismatched socks and leg warmers). In high school I finally learned to blow-dry it straight, and I abandoned my natural inclination toward ponytails for a while (I reverted later in life). At the time, I was looking to attract a boy, because I was fifteen years old and had yet to get anyone's attention—like, ever. So I copied Teri Hatcher's look from the TV show, *Lois and Clark*. It worked, I guess, because I got a boyfriend pretty soon after.

In college I discovered big hair clips, so I twirled my locks into a spiral and pulled them up against my head, clipping them near my crown and leaving a spray of hair falling over the top like a fountain. I liked this look and used it for most of my twenties. It was easy and practical for the old ballerina in me, and I somehow looked put together without having to spend more than five seconds getting it that way.

When I started losing my hair at age thirty-four, however, I told myself it was just stress (my cat dying, in particular) and that this had happened before. My hair would fall out for weeks at a time in my twenties, generally in response to a traceable traumatic occurrence like my divorce, and the loss was always temporary. Besides, I'd never lost enough to make a noticeable difference in thickness—although I always did notice a few more grays after each round.

But this time it didn't stop. I got concerned and made an appointment with a dermatologist, who combed through my hair like I had lice (although sort of in fast forward; he only did it for about ten seconds), and then announced confidently that he saw no skin issues and it should resolve soon. I walked to my car not feeling very secure in his assessment and, sure enough, that fine, thick hair that used to grow all the way down my back slowly became fine, thin hair that hung pitifully at my shoulders in drowned-rat fashion.

I was bothered, but not yet frantic. I'd perhaps lost half of my hair by the time I'd seen the dermatologist, but since I'd had so much, I still had a lot left. I decided it was just a product of my fibroid issue and would resolve after my upcoming surgery.

When you're younger, your body cooperates a lot more than it does when you're older, so my hair did exactly what I decided it would do—it eventually stopped bailing and started growing again after I recovered from my immediate health crisis. This took some time but, a year later, I was thrilled to see more thickness and little wisps blowing into the air around my face, reminding me of the flyaways I'd always had as a child that never seemed to cooperate with the rest of my ponytail. Indeed, it filled back in almost to its old thickness (although not quite), so I decided everything was okay and perhaps it would continue to fill in more over time. After all, I'd never lost that much hair before.

I turned my focus to other matters until I got really sick again and my hair started showing up on my clothes … and my pillow … and the floor. I told myself the same story I always had (stress, temporary, blah blah blah), but it was when my hair started to fall out in clumps that I thought maybe my body's behavior could no longer be predicted in the same way as before. Maybe I really was getting older now, or maybe something was really wrong.

Showers became my least favorite time of day, because it was then that I had to stare straight into my hair loss and confront it. So I took baths as often as my oily scalp allowed. Sure, I was starting to pick long pieces of fallen hair off my face and my back all day long, with some of the pieces half brown and half gray. Okay, that had happened before. Sure, I was pulling a handful of hair out of my brush every morning. But I'd pulled hair out of my brush my entire life. What I *wasn't* used to was the clump of hair that clogged the drain, detaching more and more as I moved through my shower. I'd grab some toilet paper, pull the wad out of the drain, and flush it down the toilet. I'd pretend it was all going to be okay.

But then came my hair pick.

My mother always used picks on her wet hair and so I grew up using them too. Picks are those weirdly shaped combs with extra-long fingers that sometimes the boys in high school would purposely stick in their hair. I'd always had a thing about combing my hair with a pick after I got out of the shower because I just didn't like the uncomfortable feeling of a tangled, wet mess. I'd done it for as long as I had memories, and that uncomfortable feeling won out over what happened, now, when I did it.

I'd open the drawer and pull out my sad little pick with the broken finger on the end, and carefully draw it through my towel-dried hair. For most of my life, I'd just lose a couple of strands during this process. But in my late thirties, I now found my pick getting stuck. And that is to say, so much hair would fall out and attach itself to the pick that when I went to take another stroke, the orphan hair would grab on to the rest of my hair and lift it up near the top of my head. I'd push through it anyway, making my four to six strokes, and then prepare myself for the damage.

The first step was to pull the hair off the pick and stick it in the trash (how much was there today?). The second step was to reach back, grasp my hair in my hand at the base of my neck, and draw my hand down to the bottom to remove all of the lost hair that had already dislodged itself from my head but was still mixed in with the rest (how big was *that* handful today?).

I am not a vain woman. I have mentioned I live in ponytails, and I might also mention that I continued to use the makeup a Clinique lady put me in at age seventeen for ten straight years after that. So I have never put much emotion into beauty products or fashion. But I sure cried from time to time over my hair.

It wasn't just that it was thin; I cried because it was now so thin that I could see my scalp. I was afraid to wear it down because there was no thickness to prop it off my head (flat is harsh), and I began to think I was walking around with a spotlight on my noodle now that I'd lost three-fourths of what had been there. It was a dramatic, heartbreaking time in my life.

My hair continued to fall out at this rate over the course of more than eight months and by the end of things, I was almost to the point of buying head scarves and investing in hats. But by the time my hair started regrowing a little, my distress and embarrassment gave way to some lessons that were far beyond hair.

The experience taught me, like all of my illnesses have taught me, that there are truly two truths in life about the physical body. The first is that physical beauty, if you have it (lucky you!), is fleeting. The second is that sometimes you don't understand how the outside doesn't matter until you find yourself trapped inside a broken shell.

Over time I began to manage my distress such that I was still highly concerned (and afraid I'd eventually become bald), but it became less of a focus and less of a catastrophe. Okay, so I become bald. Possible, although not probable. So what? Am I going to let it change how I feel or how I interact with the world? Or am I going to choose a different outcome?

∅ ∅ ∅

When something goes wrong in your own life or with your own body, you start looking for kindred spirits. If you have acne, you look for acne. If you have a tummy leftover from childbirth, you look for other tummies. You want to not feel alone and you want to not feel like an anomaly. So I started looking for thin hair. And when I did, I noticed that more women have it than I'd ever thought did. I also noticed that they either embraced it and carried on, or they didn't and seemed to hang their heads.

And really, the hair thing is sort of a metaphor for anything in life that is physical and uncontrollable. The ones who embrace what happens to them have a glow you notice more than this "thing" about them that maybe isn't perfect. You quickly move on from whatever that thing is—arthritis, wrinkles, a larger waistline—and on to *them*.

I asked my husband probably fifty times over the course of that experience if my hair was getting too thin, if it was noticeable, etc. etc. etc. He always told me it wasn't as noticeable as I claimed it to be, and that I focused on it more than others did. And this is usually the case with any physical change or limitation we don't like about ourselves as we get older—we see it more than anyone else does.

Losing my hair was good for me because it made me stop caring about it for a while. In fact, I stopped caring about what I looked like at all because I was physically broken in so many ways. Yes, I still wanted to look pretty and put together, but I also had a new knowledge that my appearance meant a lot less than I thought it had. So I now walked more confidently without makeup and with my failing hair, because my energy was limited and I needed it for healing—not for prepping myself just to go to the store for food. I took that leftover energy and put it into examining who I was (inside) and who I wanted to be (to the world).

🍂 🍂 🍂

We put ourselves through a lot of misery when we try to control things about getting older that we can't control. Things like changing waistlines, decreasing energy levels, failing memory, wrinkles around the eyes, and hair that maybe is still thick but is a whole lotta gray. Some of us try everything we can to fight this process instead of just letting it be. I don't think there's any harm in doing things that make you feel good about yourself, but I think the balance gets tipped when we focus so much on those things that *not* doing them causes us misery and lack of acceptance—or causes a lack of focus on the things that are more important in life.

Our bodies are just carriers of our spirits. It's natural to want to hang on to youthfulness, health, energy, and vitality. It's also natural for some of those things to fall away as we move through many decades, with our bodies eventually becoming worn out like old shoes.

I hope my hair grows back, but if it doesn't, I will adapt. I will continue to love what I've been given, and I will be grateful to be here for another year to learn and to love and to contribute. What I want to grow, instead, is me.

PEER PRESSURE

*M*ost of us remember peer pressure as something we dealt with in middle school or high school, or sometimes in college, and a lot of times it's associated with harmful things like drugs or drinking or skipping school. But I think there are two truths to peer pressure: the first is that it's not always negative, and the second is that it doesn't end in childhood.

We live in really divided political times right now, where everyone wants to see things only from their own point of view. It's a sort of herd mentality. We gather together with people who see the world like we do, who agree with us, who encourage us in our approach, and who cheer us on as one of their tribe. I think it's perfectly natural for humans to do this, but I also think we sometimes lose sight of what being carried along with a group actually does to our sense of self.

Now, there are times when it's really good to be carried along with a group. If you've decided to become part of a volunteer group and the other members encourage you to volunteer more, then you're being peer pressured into something positive for the world. Similarly, if you're told by your spouse to eat more healthfully and to put down that cheeseburger, you're being peer pressured into a longer life.

But other times it's not so good. I think as adults, we can lose touch with the dark side of peer pressure—especially when the pressuring group is full of people we perceive to be positive influences. They might be our work colleagues, our church groups, our friends, our families. Sometimes people can pressure us into the most damaging of circumstances, or can even turn us off to the truths that lie quietly inside of us. And the problem with this is that we can lose our authenticity. We can take on the beliefs of the people around us and wear them like cloaks, or hold them in front of us like shields, and find ourselves unable to see or respond to those who are different. Or we might be unable to truly reach into our own souls to figure out who we are as people, because we have to focus so hard on being the people others want us to be.

❧ ❧ ❧

One of the great accomplishments of life, so they say, is to become comfortable in your own skin, to love yourself, to be unabashedly you. And I think you can only do this if you can let go of peer pressure and instead allow yourself to *be*. Because you can never settle into who you are if you're constantly measuring yourself against the thoughts of others. Against the group. Against the herd.

I think in my own quest to set myself free from this cycle, I've often failed in the end because I resisted pressure from one direction while succumbing to pressure from a different one. For example, I never drank a single drop of alcohol until I got divorced at twenty-six. On the one hand, I didn't succumb to the pressure of friends to just have a little something from the bar; on the other hand, I fell into line with my church because I was told it was morally wrong to drink. I never stepped back and made the decision myself, really. I was just pulled into abstinence because the church was a stronger force in that tug of war.

I think I turned a corner when I asked myself one day at age twenty-eight, after I quit abusing alcohol to cope with the pain of my divorce, *Do I like alcohol or do I not like alcohol? What do I say and think about it, not what do others say and think?* And the truth was, I'd actually grown to like wine quite a bit. I liked the warmth in my chest, I liked the depth and richness (or lightness and fruitiness), and I liked that it mellowed me out on my most anxious of days. I also liked the fresh sugar/rum/mint mixture of mojitos, and I enjoyed icy margaritas with chips and salsa on a hot summer day.

The next question I asked myself was, *How much alcohol do I enjoy?* And this is where I was able to break out of peer pressure completely—I decided I liked alcohol, but not too much. I liked one drink or fewer most of the time, and I didn't want one every day or even every week. I generally liked to drink socially, but even on those days, I sometimes just wanted a Coca-Cola. And from that point on it didn't matter what anyone said or did—I wouldn't drink more than one alcoholic beverage if I didn't want to.

This is just one example from my life, but there are so many peer pressure breakthroughs I've made along the way as I've figured out who "me" is, and have let go of the forces that try to put me into a box or into a single file line. What clothes do I actually like? What time do I prefer to go to bed these days? How many people do I want to be around at one time? What foods do I enjoy? What do I want to do as a career? What size home is right for me?

I think peer pressure has its place. However, I also think we need to make room within ourselves for free thought and discovery outside of the boundaries of friends, family, and large groups. Only then can we figure out what is unique and special about us, and what really brings us joy. When we get to this place of strength, then we can measure any peer pressure against our own internal scale and decide what we actually think is best, instead of just being pulled into a tug-of-war ditch.

But we should also learn, if we are mature, to give weight to the pressure when it comes from someone important in our lives. Sometimes we need it to make necessary changes that we can't see for ourselves. That spouse who wants you to stop eating cheeseburgers to save your health? They probably have the right idea, even if you feel like you love cheeseburgers. Make sure your internal scale doesn't have too big of an ego.

MOVING ON FROM
THE GRUDGE

When we're children, we're like gnats. Something upsets us and we cry for a little bit, maybe stomp our feet on the ground, and then we turn our attention to something else. Maybe the sun is shining and we want to claim the empty swing on the playground, or maybe dinner is on the table and we're hungry, or perhaps the bubble bath is frothing near the edge of the porcelain tub and we can't wait to jump in with our action figures.

As children, our minds focus on what is immediately in front of us because we don't have the time or space to process our hurts over and over again. We lack the capacity to ruminate and replay and call up anger from our guts, whereas when we're adults, the hurt wells up in our throats and finally spills over as sobs into a big glass of wine. But as our brains grow in size and our intellects blossom, we learn how to hang on to things for a longer period of time—even things that happened as children and that we released in the moment. Sometimes we cling to memories to process what happened, because we want to understand, but sometimes we do it to absorb a lesson, so we *don't* do it again. Other times, I think, we do it because we can't see the sun shining, the dinner in front of us, the warm bath waiting at the end of a long day.

I've known a few people who are professional grudge holders, but moreover I think harboring the occasional grudge is a natural part of the human experience. If you read history books or fiction stories, you'll find mighty tales of vengeance and justice for wrongdoings. Humans seem to struggle with letting what's done and processed be done and processed. Oftentimes we can't shift our focus away from the "thing" that happened and instead funnel the negative energy into another part of our lives. So the thing takes up residence in our brains, growing twisted roots all over its surface and snuffing out all the oxygen.

❦ ❦ ❦

I held a grudge for probably ten years about being fired from a job. I was fired early on a Monday morning, at the very beginning of a pay period. I'd been unhappy in said job for a long while because of many of the things women face in the workplace: not being taken seriously, not getting promised promotions (and watching them being handed to men instead), not being treated as an equal ... things like that. I'd grown resentful about it over time, especially since I was working as hard as I thought I could, so I'm sure my negative attitude contributed to the events that eventually unfolded. But I still didn't feel like I deserved being escorted out like a criminal, coerced into signing an "I won't sue you or talk about this" agreement in order to get another paycheck in the form of severance, and being told things "just weren't working out."

I held this fury inside of me for a long time because that Monday morning became the first day of the most hopeless period of my life. I was actively suicidal, and on one dark evening I thought maybe I'd try to do something about it. I'd lost my home, I'd lost my dignity, I'd lost my ability to believe in better days, and now I'd lost my will to live. It turns out I was just too chicken to follow through.

When you are hit with an event that causes your life to completely derail, it's very easy to seethe and ruminate. It's tempting to let it take hold in your brain, to blame it, to want retribution, to want a right for the way you've been wronged, or to hold on tight until you've squeezed something out of it in your favor.

It's taken a lot of hindsight to move on from that experience and, even today, I still feel flashes of anger lodged in small pockets of my brain. This is the one big grudge of my adult life. For over a decade, in fact, I wasn't able to do anything about it except let time keep moving and wait for myself to accumulate more wisdom.

People say anger destroys *you* instead of the person or thing you are begrudging. I get that, and I think most of us get it, but this saying comes from the intellectual side of ourselves; the side of our brains that can explain situations to us with logic and impartiality.

The emotional side of our brains is a bit harder to regulate.

As I've grown older, I've learned to harness my intellectual side and use it to tame my out of control emotions. It's a skill you have to develop, I think, where you reason away some of the feelings you know are bad for you and can't beat down any other way. I told myself over the years that this one event was a necessary defining moment in my life's trajectory. I think reframing it as a necessity has gotten me through many a dark day, especially when my career has stalled out and I've questioned what I'm actually doing with my days. And maybe it's total bullshit, but maybe it really isn't, because that single event led me on a search to figure out what was next.

The unemployed period of my life lasted for fourteen months and after it was over, I found myself sleep driving to an elementary school before sunrise to greet my students as a fifth-grade teacher. I never thought I'd become one and yet it was something I'd fantasized about quietly for a large part of my life. My grandmother was the first Hispanic principal in Houston and she'd had a Ph.D. in education. My mother was a schoolteacher and so were most of my aunts. It was in my blood, I thought, and so I followed that desire to see what I might find.

What I found was the hardest job of my life and one that didn't mesh very well with my introverted personality. But had I not been fired and desperate for a paycheck, would I have ever explored that side of myself? Would I have crammed for six months to try to regain my Spanish fluency in order to pass a test that would allow me to work as a bilingual teacher (the only teaching jobs available to alternatively certified people like me)? Would I have bravely faced those children and tried to positively affect their lives, if only for a moment, if I hadn't been desperate to eat? I don't think I would have, and what a loss that would have been. Maybe even a regret too.

We plant seeds in life everywhere we walk, with every choice we make and every action we take. One of the seeds during my time as a bewildered non-worker was freelance writing, which turned into a full-time writing business four years later. Another dream come true. So every time I feel those parts of my brain light up with anger, I flip the coin intellectually and analyze how positively that event shaped my life.

❧ ❧ ❧

One would hope that by midlife, we could learn how to better manage our feelings and process our hurts. But so many of us don't, and I think it's prudent to be aware that we are all in different stages of growth. And those of us who have moved into a stage of understanding can show others, through our actions, how they can get to that place too. We can show them how we can still offer positivity and politeness even amidst unfairness and scorn. We can show them that our lives do not stop because others do not like us, do not approve of us, or do not agree with a decision we've made. We can show them that we are still willing to engage as humans if they decide to snuff out their grudge at a later date. After all, we are all part of the same human fabric that makes the earth, and one day we will all return to the same source.

But what else?

We can succeed after we get fired, turn a painful experience into something better, and then look back in gratefulness at the thing we once scorned.

LET'S TALK ABOUT BOWEL HABITS

I was on a cruise ship with my husband in the evening dining room, where they always assign seats at a table with a number of other couples who were picked, lottery-style, just for you. We were fortunate this round to have been seated next to some friendly, engaging couples with whom we shared our meals almost every day. When you find people like that, the conversation rolls out as smooth as silk.

Whenever I eat with people who don't know me, there's always some anxiety that bubbles inside because it feels like there's a spotlight on my head. My pillboxes and syringes look like a chemistry experiment gone wrong, and they also take up a respectable amount of space on the table where my water glass should be. This scene fosters glances from others at the very least, and outright questions from those who are more straightforward, and the introvert in me often feels like I have to offer an explanation just to turn the light off.

In my younger years, I would have skimmed the surface and refused to allow anyone to dive in, but these days, I'm happy to vomit out my health issues like men shoot the breeze.

"I've got a lot of issues with my stomach," I said to the couple at our cruise ship table. "I have to take all this before I eat and I can't eat certain things."

"Oh really? I have some issues too," she said, then looked to her right. "So does my husband."

"Really? Are they similar to mine?" I then explained some of the details of my symptoms and limitations.

"Well, actually ...."

The great thing about having conversations with new people is that you can feel each other out. You learn very quickly how much they are willing to share and how much you can safely share with them. In this instance, so began a shameless and matter-of-fact conversation about food and restrictions and even—for a moment —bowel habits.

At the cruise ship dinner table.

🌿 🌿 🌿

I've been a member of some rare disease support groups in recent years and sometimes people will say, "I know this is TMI" or "If you don't want to share I completely understand." And I guess the whole concept of TMI is a completely foreign idea to me these days. I mean, I get that you shouldn't broadcast your personal problems to a room full of strangers or (uninvited) to your boss or to a random acquaintance. But what I mean is if you ask me a question, I have no qualms about answering it in all the detail you'd like. Because to me it's not really gory or embarrassing, it's just life.

Part of growing older, I think, is a willingness to discuss those things that used to make you blush and giggle when you were twelve. And an interesting observation I've made is that there are still some grown folks who refuse to talk about certain things, which always amuses me to an extent. What's the big deal? It's just a body, we all have one, and we all have issues with it.

I think it's kind of akin to how talking about sex used to be taboo, and probably still is in some circles. Everyone does it (or none of us would be here) but talking about it wasn't allowed for millennia. Why? I'm not saying we should be crafting romance novels in dark corners with our girlfriends, spilling intimate details about our sex lives like it's a spectacle. But why avoid talking about it to the extent we almost pretend it doesn't exist, and women don't feel comfortable asking other women innocent questions about the issues they're having or their fears about certain things?

Whenever I see a doctor, which happens a lot in my life, I spare no detail and haven't for a long while. I think I fall back onto memories of my grandmother in her last weeks on earth, where suddenly there was no room for niceties and coyness and hiding truths. She had a body and that body was breaking down, taking all of those formalities with it.

I'd been asked to help give her a sponge bath once. The nurse's assistant and I had her sitting up as best she could, her breasts hanging free from the part of her gown that still covered her lower half. I was talking to her quietly and basting her back with warm water when I noticed her head starting to droop slowly, ever so slowly, falling forward. I moved to the left a bit, holding her steady with my right hand, and her eyes were looking downward at nothing. Then her back began heaving, her lungs gasping for air, and I called for help to the assistant who was now working across the room at the sink.

As the nurses ran in and the "Code!" alarms sounded, they rushed me out like I was being pushed off a subway train. My last glimpse, just as the door shut, was of her being placed naked on the bed with all sorts of tubes and probes being attached in rapid fire. I stood alone in the hall and thought to myself how in that moment, she was not so much a person as a body. Her personality, which was locked inside there somewhere, was currently unavailable to worry about modesty or how many people were seeing her naked and undignified. All she would be worried about, if she were even aware of what was going on, was surviving.

She did survive that day and I was glad the events of the afternoon weren't the closing memories—for me—of her life. But I suppose my own struggles with my health (which began after her death) have led me to the place I thought about in the hall that day. To an understanding that I have a body to house my person, my spirit, and my personality, but that my body is not me and is sort of a machine, really. Anything that happens to it is not embarrassing, weird, gross, or to be ashamed of. It just *is*. It doesn't change who I am on the inside at all, unless I decide to let my frustration with it rule my life.

🍃 🍃 🍃

My cruise lasted seven lovely days, aside from the post-Hurricane Harvey waves we'd ridden into that sent the ship rocking like a toy (and caused us all a couple of days of intermittent, seasickness misery). And we didn't spend our entire dinners talking about bowel habits or food allergies or the other health woes that brought us together. But we did share that connection, using it as a running joke about what might happen after the meal or commiserating with one another when something we'd eaten the day before hadn't sat well.

We haven't seen that couple since the cruise ended, but we've maintained a connection to them through social media because they live about thirty minutes from us. And we have tentative plans to play tennis together when I'm in a better place. And isn't that cool? Whether we have an enduring friendship or not, we made a connection that will stick with me—one that I'll remember on every other cruise I take and that will live on in my memories from the vacation. And it was all because someone asked a question about my health, I answered, and they were open enough to share something equally "embarrassing" about theirs.

PURGING YOUR ATTACHMENTS

I had this special laundry basket all through my twenties and early thirties. It was a really sturdy, thick, smooth white plastic with a curve in the side that fit perfectly on my hip like a baby. I kept it in my closet, not only for carting laundry to and from the washer/dryer (which for a time was a couple of miles away), but also to hold my dirty clothes in between washes in a somewhat contained pile (so it served as my hamper too).

I don't remember exactly when I got this basket, but I do remember I got it from Target. I bought it to replace an old one that I'd either inherited or picked up cheaply from somewhere else, and it became one of the first new things I'd ever purchased for myself as an adult. I remember taking it to my apartment and placing it perfectly in my closet, then stepping back to study my new addition with a bit of pride. It was all mine and it was brand new too!

When I was in my mid-thirties, we moved to an apartment that had a closet with a poor configuration for my half of the space. By the time I'd put my shoes on the racks and left space in the corner for my cat's sleeping cube, there was simply no room for my favorite laundry basket at all (unless I planned to stand in it while picking out my clothes). I played Tetris in there for quite a while. I mean, I'd made it work somehow in every other place I'd lived. But in the end I was exactly where I'd started—the only place I could make it fit was right where I needed to stand. I'd simply have to find a new solution.

I got in my car rather bemoaningly, and I went back to Target. This time I was a much older adult with a bit more money available to spend on a replacement. I ran my hands over the tall, upright laundry baskets and thought about what style I might want, as these days I preferred natural materials as often as possible. But then the practical side of my brain warned that I have cats, and that natural materials often magically transform into scratching posts, so I admitted defeat and returned to the plastic options. Eventually I set my eyes on a tall, thin hamper that was made of brown plastic but that was constructed in weaves to mimic something more natural.

This was the one.

I purchased my new basket, which also had a lid on it (I'd never had one of those as an adult), and squished it into the reclined front seat of my Honda coupe. I came home and took it straight to the closet so I could break up with my faithful companion that was still as white as the day I'd gotten it. It didn't even have any scuffs! Sad, oh so sad.

I took my new brown weaved thing in and, with a quick swap, placed it in exactly the place a tall, skinny hamper needed to go. My longtime laundry basket was now on the floor behind me outside of the closet, and I looked back at it wistfully—although only for about half a second, because I felt a little sparkly inside about the new basket.

I liked it.

Shit.

I liked how it looked, I liked how it fit, I liked that it would completely conceal my dirty clothes while also returning much needed real estate to my closet. And then I thought, *Why didn't I do this a long time ago?* My new hamper worked so much better for the life I'd been living for quite some time. I no longer needed to carry clothes on my hip like a baby, because I no longer had to trek across town (or even down apartment stairs) to do my laundry. So why did I hold on to a basket that was made expressly for this purpose, rather than converting to a proper hamper when my washer/dryer was just twenty paces away, and when I didn't have the space in my home for both?

Well, it wasn't really about the basket, was it?

※ ※ ※

There is a really popular book that was published in the last few years called *The Magic of Tidying Up* by Marie Kondo. It's about minimalism and clearing out clutter. The idea is to hold on to the things you really love and toss the rest, because it's not only a waste of space to hold on to unnecessary things, but also a waste of energy. (I have not read this book so that's my interpretation of media interviews and such.) I decided this was a good philosophy to embrace in my own life, so I've really pared down my belongings to those things I really love—even parting with some of my books (gasp, horror of horrors). Probably part of this is a desire to live neatly and not be bogged down by clutter, but a lot of it is more practical; I have a small home and I just don't have room for tons of crap.

I got really good at purging over time, but it was really hard at first. People seem to hold on to stuff for a variety of reasons. I feel like most of the time they are holding on to stuff because they want to hold on to a memory. Case in point: you save your childhood records because you want to remember how you used to play them, not because you still play them or because you intend to sell them as antiques for a huge profit one day. Or, you hold on to your mother's old food storage containers because they were your mother's or because they came from another time, despite the fact that you've moved on to glass containers that don't leech petrochemicals into your blood.

Any time I see people struggle with letting go of a thing, I tell them it's really not about the *thing*. The answer to this dilemma is simple, because it's the truth: you will keep the memory of the thing (or the people or the events or the time surrounding the thing) even if you lose the actual thing. Sure, there are some items we all want to keep. I have a locket given to me by my grandmother before she died that was passed down through several generations, and I also have a stuffed animal that my father bought me before a surgery when I was seven years old. But in general, the quantity of things I'm holding on to strictly for sentimental reasons is now limited to one or two small boxes and a handful of displays on my (limited) shelves.

This mindset has translated for me in other ways as well. For example, I no longer hunt for souvenirs when I travel. I used to snatch up anything and everything that had a good price tag and that I thought would help me better "remember" my trip. But these days, I pick just one thing I actually want to use in my life—like a sterling silver turtle necklace from a stop in Jamaica that I loved at first sight and would have bought at home anyway, or some tan boots from a trip to Chicago that I adored and have worn for nearly a decade. The magic is that every time I use the thing, I remember my trip. But the secret is, I don't *have* to use this thing to remember the trip at all.

🍃 🍃 🍃

Letting go of my laundry basket was perhaps my first foray into breaking the attachment between memories and things. People often comment on how freeing it feels when they can finally let go of something they were holding on to—like when they clean out their junk closet or finally sell off their dead relatives' furniture —and I can tell you this is true for me also. I loved that white, plastic laundry basket for reasons that really had nothing to do with the basket or its function. I loved it because I'd bought it for myself and it had been a constant through so many hard times.

Naturally I felt a pang of sadness as I drove to Goodwill to donate it to another lucky son of a gun (it really was a good, sturdy basket, you guys). But then I pulled out of that parking lot and I felt free. I felt new. I felt fresh. I'd let go of something that really wasn't serving my life anymore but that I'd held on to for no other reason except to grasp at sentimentality. And I've never missed it in the years since, because I love the tall, brown hamper I still use today. Although this time I love it for the right reasons: because it fits properly in my space and helps me maintain the clutter-free home that soothes my soul.

THE CHILD INSIDE

We all have this little child inside who is sitting on the edge of our minds, legs dangling off a wall and into a blank space below. We start our lives as actual children, seeking approval, needing guidance, being steered by outside forces into a good direction (or not). We have raw emotions, we're unafraid to say how we feel, we approach the world with valor and bravery and a sense of immortality because we haven't yet learned the dangers that lurk in the shadows.

But this child remains even as we grow older, with our skin creasing and our organs weakening, or with our hair graying and our memories growing fuzzy. And as our intellect widens, so does our sphere of wisdom, but inside still sits that pure child who now bears the scars of the world. And this child is the seed from which we grew, the beginning of our lives that we've almost forgotten about because it's been so many years.

I long struggled with this child. I grew older and kept looking for things my inner child wanted when I was young (acceptance, approval, control) but that she still couldn't seem to find later in life. This child took over my adulthood in the form of rampant emotions, unchecked pain, occasional anger, and even downright despair. I wanted to be seen and to be understood. I wanted to have things finally go my way, and to move in whatever manner I chose.

But life doesn't work that way.

Sometimes we don't get what we want and sometimes we can't do what we want. Sometimes we hurt and sometimes we're angry. And in those times, the rebellion flares inside and the child's legs kick against the wall, our spirit threatening to heave itself over the edge and into the abyss, as if to relinquish its own flame would right all the wrongs we seem to have no power to correct.

❦ ❦ ❦

I've mentioned that I grew up in a broken (divorced) home which, to be honest, would not have been that big of a deal had other things turned out better in the house I got stuck in for my youth. So many grownups say they are "staying together for the kids," but I think, really, they stay together to avoid confrontation and messiness. They stay together to keep up a façade that they believe their kids will accept wholeheartedly. But kids are just mini versions of us. It takes them a while to harness their wisdom, but they have it inside already and they'll put it to use in good time.

If I'd had the love I'd needed from the single parent I was placed with, my inner child would have been content. She would have smiled at the breeze and watched the clouds floating above, perhaps lounging effortlessly on the wall with her feet propped up and her mind dreaming about the future. But because she didn't, she stewed and fought and waited to break free when she was old enough to go look for that contentment somewhere else.

Getting older means merging that inner child into who we are today. Stroking that child's cheek, soothing her hurts, whispering away the anger so that it floats off on a breeze. And then saying, "Come here and let us walk together hand in hand. We are one in the same, we always have been. You don't have to hurt anymore."

This merging happens differently for everyone. Some people find it in church, some find it in friends, some find it in their careers, some find it in their spouses. I found it in a combination of spiritual exploration, a wonderful husband, a whole lot of counseling, and some health issues that knocked me off my feet and into a place of absolute helplessness.

My inner child was soothed as I learned to accept that I was brought into this world for a purpose, and that my childhood was an integral part of that purpose. She started merging into the adult version of myself as I transformed memories of loneliness and abuse into meaningful work—the kind of meaningful work that tries to help others overcome those same obstacles (like this book). She became more peaceful as I began to understand that I am now loved unconditionally by my husband, that life never goes as planned for anyone, and that we're all part of something bigger than just our immediate circumstances. She stepped back into the shadows when I realized I can't concentrate on the past if I want to grow, because the answers don't live with the younger version of my spirit.

Once you can finally soothe that child who sits on the wall of your mind, you can break free of the bonds you have to the things in your past. You can let go of those memories or feelings that keep you from stepping forward into who you were meant to be. You can find your confidence, your voice, your spirit. You can learn to find refuge in yourself, and guidance in yourself, and direction in yourself. You are older and wiser and you don't need any outside help anymore.

You've got it all in your heart, and you have all along.

JOY IS ATTAINABLE

So many times in my life, I've felt joy was elusive. I'd hear people talk about it and would sometimes see the emotion portrayed on television, but I was pretty convinced I'd never experienced much of it myself (and also that I likely never would). As I got older and that cross-country move to a beautiful location never happened, and as that perfect job never happened, and as I watched people chase joy relentlessly from city to city or boyfriend to boyfriend, I realized that joy actually does live within everyone—it's just a matter of coaxing it out sometimes.

❧ ❧ ❧

When I was thirty-six years old, I attended my first real concert. And this is only partly true, because I'd watched Stevie Wonder the year before at an outdoor arena in Lake Tahoe as the crisp breeze blew and the sun set through the trees. But that concert had been a fortieth birthday present to my husband and was an artist I'd chosen just for him. This time, I was attending a concert for me.

I'd grown up listening to Boyz II Men's second album on repeat day after day, making them an integral part of my adolescent life. I had a crush on Wanya, but I also got lost in the group's melodies and harmonies, which were mostly about love and relationships—things I didn't know yet from my home life and therefore grasped at desperately through music. I knew every song, every note. One time I even listened to this album all the way to and from Mississippi on a road trip from Dallas we were making to visit my uncle, and again a year later on a drive to and from San Antonio.

My middle school years were a sorrowful time in my life. Times of ridicule at school, turmoil at home, deafening loneliness, and an overall failure to fit in with the world. I was tiptoeing into becoming a young lady and I spent hours dreaming of the faceless boy who might someday have a crush on my crooked-toothed self and ask me to "go with him," as we said back then. That day would be far, far off because I was one of the girls in the shadows. But Boyz II Men's perfect pitch R&B was a beautiful sound that cut through the darkness in my life.

My husband was the one who spotted the concert online when I was in my mid-thirties (and more than twenty years removed from middle school). He was sitting at his desk and told me to come look at the screen. It was going to be on a Tuesday.

"A workday," I said. "Should we? I mean, we don't stay out late on weeknights anymore. We haven't done that in a long time."

To think that I even hesitated shows how far away I'd drifted from the girl of my youth. But I feel like we all do this when life piles cinder blocks upon us. We forget the magic of the things that used to mean so much to us, and in this case, I suppose I'd blocked my favorite music group out with the other childhood memories I still wished weren't there.

"It might be fun," my husband said. "Wasn't Boyz II Men your favorite group?"

"Yeah it was my favorite group for a long time," I said. "I suppose we should go."

I *supposed* so?

Arriving at the concert felt like being swept up into a sea of not-quite-old-and-not-quite-young humans, all looking to recapture a moment in time that was long gone. I sat with my husband in the arena, perched somewhere near the top but not quite in the nosebleeds, looking at a bunch of middle-aged housewives dressed in nineties gear and heavy makeup. Their kids (they told me in the restroom) were at home with their husbands while they relieved their glory days. Me? I was reliving the highlight of my un-glory days. I was revisiting the most beautiful thing I'd had in my world for a three-year slice of my youth.

I studied the stage carefully, with its walkway all around and a big screen behind, and wondered if it was a good setup or not since I had no frame of reference. I remember checking my watch obsessively as my stomach started doing jumping jacks. *Am I nervous? What's this? I should be excited; why do I feel nervous?*

As the clocked ticked and they prepared to come on, I lost my grip on the present and was swept away by a wave of sorts, flying straight backward and landing squarely in my youth. The intensity of my old feelings about the music returned and my adrenaline kicked in, flushing red to my cheeks and pounding my heart in my chest. I couldn't believe I was about to be in the same room with these men who I'd adored for so long. Suddenly it was almost more than I could take. As the lights dimmed and a familiar song started up in the background, my jumping jacks turned to somersaults and then fireworks. Women started screaming, I started screaming. And this is where I had my first experience with *joy*.

Joy is your insides bursting into a puff of confetti. The rest of the world dims and you find yourself in a quiet sort of place that feels like suspended animation. You forget about illness, death, politics, global warming, family dysfunction, divorce, terrorist attacks. You're so laser focused on the moment and on the joy that there is no before or after, there is only now.

What happened to me on the outside as I was going through this internal experience probably looked a bit silly or juvenile, which I cared nothing about. I remember jumping up and down, screaming, squealing. Then hiding my head bashfully on my husband's shoulder, screaming again, jumping up and down again. I felt like a two-year-old discovering colorful balloons. And then all of a sudden and quite unexpectedly came the tears. I cried tears of joy.

When you've been through what feels like a lifetime of heartache, all you really know are tears of sorrow. You think you may have cried from happiness on occasion, but joy? It feels like a false emotional state made up by glass-half-full kinds of people who have never been dragged through the mud. And I truly believe that the feeling of joy is foreign to half of humanity, especially when we consider the entire world and all of the bad things that go on in it for so many groups of people. So many of them live in sorrow and fear, and when you're in that place, you cannot have joy. I was part of that group.

As Wanya got on his knees to pour his voice into the microphone and fill the auditorium with song, I cried some more. In fact, my husband told me later that he almost cried watching me cry (my husband does not cry) because he had never seen me experience so much joy. True joy is contagious by default, I also learned that night.

The thing is, we all have the capacity to feel joy even if we've never felt it before or barely know it's possible. My joy was not coming from Wanya or Nathan or Shawn, or from "On Bended Knee" being sung live in my presence. My joy was coming from how I reacted to those people and those songs. It was what my insides—my mind, my soul—did with those things and with the experience I was having in the moment. And this tells me that joy is possible for everyone, although maybe the formula has to be just right for some of us before we can find it.

I walked out of that concert a different human being because I'd attained what I had previously believed was completely unattainable. I felt soothed and whole and fully human, at least for a moment in time.

I've tiptoed around joy since then but I've never quite reached that level again, and I know now that it's not because I'm incapable. It's because I haven't learned how to fully trigger my own innate feelings of joy. You know, the ones that lie dormant and are drawn out by something like a Boyz II Men concert when you're thirty-six years old because you aren't able to access them on your own.

Finding joy that day changed my perspective on what is possible for the human experience—even for those of us who don't come from loving homes or happy childhoods, who go through illness and divorce and famine, who experience loss and hurt and betrayal. We are all capable of feeling so much happiness that our spirits want to burst from our bodies and disperse into the air.

I look back on this concert with a smile and a warmth in my chest, because it is still the pinnacle of joy in my life. I hope I get to that place again one day, even if it takes years of personal growth to tap into my own internal joy on more of an on-demand basis. Figuring out how to find it amidst the rubble of my life will be more than worth the work.

LESSONS FROM LILY

*L*ily is my newest rescue cat. She's one in a short line of rescues I've taken in since college, because I've been fortunate enough to spend many years with each one (I keep two at a time) before having space for another. She's been the most challenging by far, and she's also taught me a lot about life.

Animals are really good at reminding us to live in the moment and to not get too far ahead of ourselves, because that is all they are capable of doing. When they're eating, they're not fretting about where the next meal is coming from. They're enjoying their food. When it's sunny outside, they bask in the warmth instead of bemoaning the cloudy days that came before, or the ones that might come after. And when they're hurt—as happened to my Lily—they find grace and contentment with whatever is in front of them, even if it's absolutely life altering and seemingly catastrophic from the human perspective.

Lily tore her ACL in a fit of unnecessary panic one night in my house. I walked into the room with the lights off, she didn't recognize me, and something happened when she tried to flee that ripped her leg inside and left it mostly unusable. It was a horrible night in my memory, but one that shouldn't have been entirely unexpected. Panic seems to be a part of Lily's DNA and it's either based on some sort of previous trauma (my feeling, because she has certain triggers) or something gone awry in her wiring.

🍃 🍃 🍃

I found Lily by doing a search online on one of those adoption sites, after having just lost my beloved nineteen-year-old rescue who had been with me since college. Lily hadn't found a forever home because she'd been too frightened to interact with anyone who came to visit while she was in foster care. As the other kitties got adopted, Lily's stay turned into weeks ... and then months ... and then years. By the time I arrived to meet her, she was nearing three years old and hadn't had one single person interested in becoming her mama.

I've never taken in a cat who appeared to hate me. I remember very clearly the way she was when I met her, a rather small gray and white ball of fluff hunched against the wall, pupils wide, chin tucked, meatloaf position but with her rear limbs at the ready to move quickly. She had a look of terror splashed all over her face, and I dared not flinch as she stared at me from behind an invisible wall.

Over two different visits at her foster mom's house, I worked slowly to try to make a connection. I'd talk to her and try to inch closer, and she'd flee to another part of the room. I'd do it again and hope for success, having been a sort of animal whisperer all my life, but she'd dart off behind the TV stand. Had I lost my touch? The foster mom also tried holding her in her lap so I could at least run a finger across her cheek, but Lily's pupils just got wider as I moved closer. She struggled to free herself although seemed to understand that the human was stronger than she was. I eventually got to touch her, but she didn't like it at all.

I took her home anyway.

Something about Lily felt divinely planned. It seemed like she was supposed to be with me even though I had no actual evidence that either of us would benefit from the arrangement. But to my surprise, it only took a few days for her to come around while confined to the second bathroom. The moment she suddenly flopped over in her cubby, purring as I pet her head, is one I'll cherish for the rest of my life. And now I can see her purpose unfolding before me every day she's with me, because she's one of my soulmates.

🌿 🌿 🌿

Lily's accident was only about a month into our time together, and aside from it being terribly timed (my husband and I had just moved into our first house and I'd also just lost my job), it required a very expensive surgery followed by eight weeks of cage rest. I went out and bought a wire dog kennel that was just big enough to fit her litter box, a bed, food, and water, and, with tears in my eyes, took it all home to put together. We set it up in the master bathroom to create a quiet space where she could feel safe. This would be her life while she healed with her leg in a little cast, and I was absolutely distraught about it.

Lily had been a very active kitty because she was still young and hadn't lost all of her kitten personality. It hurt my heart because she now limped and was unable to move around—and worse, she wouldn't be able to get out of four walls of bars now. She couldn't hide (she still did that often), couldn't run (she's the fastest cat I've ever had), couldn't climb or jump (she once got on top of the kitchen cabinets and we couldn't get her down). She also couldn't cuddle up with me in bed at night with her little face smooshed against mine.

After I brought her home from surgery, there was a short adjustment period that was mostly consumed by rest and being high on pain medication. When that passed, it was clear she didn't like the cage or the cast, but in a very short time she somehow became okay with it. Instead of rebelling against her confinement and thrashing around, she seemed to instead focus on the good moments that came. She took joy in me sitting with her so much and petting her head. She watched the squirrels and birds on YouTube with fascination, which I kept running on a laptop almost 24/7 to help with boredom. She relished the ten to fifteen minutes she was allowed out of the cage twice a day, staying present in every second and not really thinking about having to go back in there. It was like all was well in the world despite her dramatically altered existence.

This is not to say that she didn't have her moments. Every night, from about eight o'clock until eleven, she'd experience her most difficult times because her circadian rhythm roused her into an active state in which she couldn't indulge. But—as I was, probably serendipitously, unemployed—I would sit with her, play with her, talk to her. I'd spray a calming pheromone spray, much like humans use essential oils or hot baths, and she'd settle back down in her bed. I passed my days seated on a pillow on the bathroom floor outside of her cage, and she passed hers on that soft bed, drifting in and out of sleep while watching the animals on the computer screen.

🍃 🍃 🍃

I've learned so much from Lily just as an observer. First, she lost so much in such a short time. That's a hard thing for any of us to process. And even though she would eventually regain her mobility and her freedoms, *she* didn't know it. All she knew was the reality that existed—that her life was now lived in a cage, and there was this blasted annoying thing on her leg that she couldn't shake off. And somehow it was enough, because she was going to enjoy those pets and kisses and brushes, and those animals on the computer screen, and the time out of her cage that she was allowed, and forget about the rest.

I take those lessons as I move through my own life and struggles. My situation is a bit different in that I feel permanently stuck in a cage sometimes, but perhaps I can approach it in the same way. When I can't write at any time of day like I used to, because my health and medications sometimes make it harder to do so as the day goes on, perhaps I can take joy in writing during the mornings when my brain is clear. When I can't practice yoga at all, which has happened fairly often over the past several years, perhaps I can be content in being able to take an evening walk. When I get tired and it's only one o'clock in the afternoon, because that's just life with a chronic health condition sometimes, maybe I can find acceptance that this is just the way it's going to be. And maybe I can enjoy a show on Netflix rather than wallow in my inability to move.

Also, perhaps I can stop living in a world of catastrophes. I'm really good at imagining the worst outcomes for my life even if they are minuscule possibilities. If Lily had done what I was doing, she'd have fallen into a swirling pit of despair about living in a cage for the rest of her life (which wasn't actually going to happen) and having a cast on her leg that kept her from moving around (which wasn't going to happen, either). She'd have gotten lost in the sorts of thoughts I have every day: *What if my health gets worse? What if I can't bring in enough income? What if we can't make our mortgage payment one day? What if a tornado comes and destroys everything we have? What if one of my kitties—or my husband—dies?*

Humans are both blessed and cursed to be able to think in such depths and abstractions. The problem is, those thoughts can prevent us from enjoying the moment or the blessings we are given in the midst of hard times. It certainly happens to me. I wasn't able to fully enjoy the time I was given to take care of Lily when she was injured because I was so worried about where my income would come from and how we were going to pay off the thousands of dollars in vet bills.

❦ ❦ ❦

As I write this, I've decided I'm going to move forward in life and not only use Lily, but all animals, as examples of how to live in the present and find contentment regardless of the situation. I actually saw a video two days ago of a sweet pit bull who had been paralyzed from the waist down, losing the use of his back legs. Normally I don't watch videos like these because they squeeze my heart so badly, but in this case, I saw an amazingly joyful pooch. He pulled himself down the hallway with his two working legs, his broken ones dragging behind him, and approached the camera with a broad smile spread across his face. When he got his wheelchair and was able to use it, that joy blossomed into a burst of happiness that settled on everyone around him. He wasn't focused on what he couldn't do; he was focused on what he *could* do. So when his life improved with the chair, he just went from happy to happier rather than from sad to happy.

As we move through life, we can all be better than— or at least as good as—these animals at embracing the present, don't you think?

HOME IS ...

I returned recently from a trip to the Florida coast, a place I love to visit because the blues and greens that are punctuated by birds and breezes lull me into a happy mental place. I don't get to visit often because there are just so many physical places in the world to go—and I also am not a trust fund baby with infinite travel funds (alas). But I noticed something different this time that I hadn't seen in myself during prior visits: I came home just as happy as I'd been while I was there, and as I'd been before I'd left.

The last time I'd been to Florida was maybe two years prior and it was my first real visit in many years. I'd fallen in love with the place (granted, it wasn't the middle of summer when it's an inferno) and upon returning home, declared myself utterly depressed and despondent to be once again surrounded by concrete and cars. My blues lasted a week or so before I pulled myself out, with residual effects persisting for at least a month as I reminisced through photos and watched videos I'd taken, and researched Florida online until my eyes started to lose focus. I wanted to go back. And I also felt like it was so much better than my current home.

Home is not really a destination, though. It took me a long time to realize that the feeling of "home" is something you carry around with you all the time, like a sapling. You just plant it into the ground wherever you happen to end up, and it takes root until it's time to move again. It can't really be left behind and it's not really in any particular destination, although, yes, having a roof over your head is sort of essential to the process.

When I think about a home, I think about a place that's mine (or that feels like it's mine even if it's owned by a landlord). It's where I rest my body, where I find refuge from the world, where my loved ones live, and where I house my worldly possessions. There are a lot of other things that make up the sense of "home," such as community and activities and even the weather, but ultimately I've come to believe that the biggest part of what makes a place home is simply the way you feel about it.

🍂 🍂 🍂

I've noticed a lot of people move away to escape from something, which I wanted to do many times over in my twenties and early thirties. They call it a "change of scenery" or a "fresh start" as a way to distract from the deeper unhappiness they can't seem to resolve in their spirit. The idea is that changing the outside will somehow change the inside or offer a new perspective, which I think is a farce most of the time.

When I was in my twenties, I used to get lectures from people older than me about how you can't run away from yourself and how "you" will follow you wherever you go. I pushed the idea away and insisted that it didn't apply to me, setting a goal for myself of moving out of state by age thirty-five if I weren't married and life wasn't going my way. I thought if I could move, then I'd somehow find what was missing. Maybe I'd fill the hole in my heart or the void in my existence. It seemed as if so many of the problems I was facing simply *had* to be riding on the location where I resided, because I couldn't seem to resolve them any other way.

Luckily for me I was married by age thirty-five, so when that birthday came, I didn't bolt off into the sunset after randomly spinning a globe to determine which direction to go. Still, I felt like something in my life was broken that was tied to my current place. So I pined to get away from it and rejected my current home in favor of a mystical one that didn't really exist.

By the time I left for this most recent trip to Florida, I was viewing life through a different lens. I'd gone through two years of serious illness where I was locked inside of my home most of the time, lying heavy on the couch or struggling to get out of bed in the morning. And I'd come to understand that where I live has nothing to do with the city in which my house was built. That I can like my home and be content in it, no matter where it happens to be, and that I can also appreciate my visits to places that appeal to me and that I might like to have surround me one day.

I observed in myself a full and happy heart upon my return from my trip to Florida, and not a hint of situational depression or bemoaning of concrete. I was both happy to have visited a placed I longed to be and happy to return to the place I currently called my home (Texas). Instead of obsessing online about how to scheme my way into a cross-country move like I might have done before, I resumed the rhythm of my current life while keeping a warm dream in the back of my mind.

Part of figuring out life is figuring out the things you really want to do, the places you want to go, and the person you want to be. I think this process becomes clouded when you place too much emphasis on the external as a means to securing happiness. Because most of the time, there is nothing external that can fix the problems in your life; there are only things that can enhance it and make what you already have even better. It's sort of like fanning flames so that they grow and spread, but you'd need to have already lit the fire yourself.

One day I do want to live within driving distance to some sort of water. I want a huge, screened-in porch and a big garden out back. I want to look over and see my scruffy Maine Coon rescue cat (the one who *didn't* mangle his leg) sprawled across the floor in the breeze, or perched in one of those ugly cat trees, eyeing some small birds as they flutter around a feeder. I want to spend my weekends taking chairs and an umbrella to the beach, watching the ocean and the surfers, looking for dolphins that soar mightily out of the water and flop back in with a splash. I want to take pictures of the seaweed and the gulls, the shells and the foam, the grasses and the flowers.

None of this is necessary for me to have a good life, though; it would just add to the life I already have and build upon my feelings about what already is. And the truth is that if I never make it because I get hit by a bus or because my wallet simply won't allow it, I can still find my peace anyway. I can still have contentment in my life anyway. It's already inside of me and has been all along—and it isn't dependent on the city outside my windows.

IT TAKES COURAGE
TO BE YOU

When I was trying to find myself in my creative work, I tried to emulate the things and people who were already out there. I looked at what Hemingway did, at what Stephen King did, at what Elizabeth Gilbert did, at what Mitch Albom did. I tried to figure out how I could do some version of that for myself, because I was having trouble finding my own voice and style. Now these are all very different writers and their books are nothing alike, but in my mind they had a common thread: they were all successful and they were all skilled at their craft. This was important to me because I didn't want to be successful for success's sake. I wanted to be successful because I was skilled at what I was doing and because I had something good to offer to the world. So I examined their work and their lives, searching endlessly for something I could translate into my own world that would help propel me along.

I first noticed I enjoyed writing when I was in college, working on research papers for my many, many lit classes.

This enjoyment continued in my twenties and thirties as I built my personal blog, splaying my heart out for the entire internet to judge if it so desired. Sometimes I could sit down and spill out pages upon pages of words in a very short time, and words that actually made sense and formed a cohesive whole. People responded positively and I personally thought some of it was pretty good. But there was never anything that was good *enough*—not like those other writers. Not like the ones who were paid to write books and share their stories, whether personal or completely made up. I couldn't do *that*; I just vomited my thoughts and emotions and observations about the world. But I think, honestly, all artists have a whisper in their brains that says, *you're an imposter,* and it goes on for the entirety of their lives.

❦ ❦ ❦

I was thinking the other day about how it really takes courage to be you. When we are truly ourselves, we lie naked and exposed. We can be deeply hurt and have our entire sense of selves shattered if what we are putting out there is rejected as not good enough by the world, or if it is labeled as weird, or if it is said to be unacceptable. I admire Lady Gaga for being different and I find it refreshing that she has the confidence to be who she is. But at the same time, I scratched my head when she wore that dress made out of raw meat. And I know others did too, because it's been years and I still remember the story and the vocal backlash.

If that had been me, how would I have absorbed the criticism? Would it have shaken me to my core? Or would I have been strong enough in my sense of self to let it roll off and drain away in the gutter?

Sometimes it takes a long time, years or decades, to finally settle in to that person who we actually are—and to be comfortable and confident. We hide behind trends and norms, fear and insecurity, or a simple desire to fit in. We feel like if we're truly ourselves, we'll somehow lose our place in the world. We won't be allowed to be amongst the rest of humanity, swimming along in a large school that's heading somewhere toward the horizon. And because we feel these things and we hide in this way, we become unable to stay in touch with who we were meant to be. And we miss out on living a life that would bring us the most joy.

Michelangelo, Hemingway, Elvis Presley, Oprah, Neil deGrasse Tyson. These are all people who we look at and say, "Wow they were/are unique." They are different, they are refreshing, and they are successful too. On the whole, these people have been accepted by society for their uniqueness and even embraced because of it. Someone always has to be the first or the one and only. These people chose to be who they were, to be true to themselves, and as a consequence they became revered and loved.

We "little" people stare at these "big" people from afar and try to figure out what in them we can find in us. We pick those who have done the things we wish to do, or who have the lives we wish to have, and we try to create a carbon copy of those traits for ourselves. We want to have a little slice of that success or of that life. We want to be accepted and lauded for who we are, even if emulating others means we aren't actually ourselves anyway.

It *does* take a lot of courage to be you. And part of this courage is what it takes to keep striving to figure out who "you" really is. It's taken me a long time to decide that spewing my thoughts and feelings and observations is who I truly am. I wanted to be a fiction novelist for many, many years. And I tried many, many times. I failed once, and then I failed again, and again after that. Now this is not to say I will never become a novelist because there is a part of me that still wants to try, but it wasn't until I really examined who I was that I finally started focusing on writing the things I was supposed to write. The things that came naturally to me. The things that brought me peace.

And writing my stories was scary, because they weren't like the stories I'd read by my favorite authors. But they were mine and I enjoyed them, and they worked because they were what I would have wanted to read if I were to search for a book that spoke to me. So I decided I was just going to be me and see what the world thought of it. If they didn't like it, oh well. *I liked it*. And while I know I'm not impervious to criticism and that society's rejection of me as a person would still feel devastating on the inside, I also know I've gotten to the point where I *must* try to be who I am.

🍃 🍃 🍃

There is a saying in life that goes something like, "We stay the same until doing so is more painful than changing." I think a number of us hit this wall at different times in our lives when we decide we can't stand something for one more minute. But what we do next is the interesting part. How do we change, how do we evolve, how do we choose what to do with ourselves and with our time? Do we keep trying to repeat what hasn't worked before … or do we try something new?

There is another saying too, which I like, that says, "The definition of insanity is doing the same thing and expecting different results." Do you want to be insane? Or do you want to be you? Do you want to go on trying to do the thing you're not meant to do, and be the person you aren't meant to be, simply to please others or to achieve some illusive standing in life?

I choose sanity these days. I choose to evolve and to grow and to do the things I'm meant to do while I still have time to do them.

I choose, finally, to be me.